Never Too Late

A COMEDY IN THREE ACTS

By Sumner Arthur Long

SAMUEL FRENCH, INC.
25 West 45th Street NEW YORK 36
7623 Sunset Boulevard HOLLYWOOD 46
LONDON *TORONTO*

PRINTED IN U. S. A.

NEVER TOO LATE, by Sumner Arthur Long, was originally produced at The Playhouse, N. Y. C., Nov. 27, 1962, by Elliott Martin and Daniel Hollywood, under the direction of George Abbott, with the following cast:

(*In order of appearance*)

GRACE KIMBROUGH .... *Leona Maricle*
HARRY LAMBERT .... *Paul Ford*
EDITH LAMBERT .... *Maureen O'Sullivan*
DR. JAMES KIMBROUGH .... *House Jameson*
CHARLIE .... *Orson Bean*
KATE .... *Fran Sharon*
MR. FOLEY .... *Wallace Engelhardt*
MAYOR CRANE .... *John Alexander*
POLICEMAN .... *Ed Griffith*

All the action of the play takes place in the living room of the Lambert home in Calverton, Massachusetts.

ACT ONE

SCENE 1: *A Summer Sunday, around noon.*
SCENE 2: *The next day, around six-thirty in the evening.*

ACT TWO

SCENE 1: *Almost six o'clock in the evening, a few days later.*
SCENE 2: *Saturday, about noon.*

ACT THREE

Late that night.

NOTICE TO AMATEUR AND STOCK PRODUCERS: Where the title of this play appears in programs, posters, billboards and houseboards, *credit must be given* to the author, to Elliott Martin and Daniel Hollywood as producers, and to George Abbott as director, of the original New York production. Scene designs, lighting designs, costume plots and music from the original New York production of this play are not available.

Never Too Late

ACT ONE

Scene 1

Scene: *We are in the home of* Harry Lambert—*of Calverton, Mass. It is the large living room of a substantial two-story structure with a spacious green lawn sweeping up to its front porch. Being the oldest house in the neighborhood gives added prestige to its existence.* Harry Lambert *takes great pride in the fact that they don't build homes like his any more, and nobody knows better than he. For* Harry Lambert *supplies most of Calverton's lumber. He owns the largest lumberyard in town. The living room is an extension of* Harry's *personality. It is neither happy nor sad, but is comfortable and durable. A simple but attractive staircase Up Center semi-winds to the second floor and various bedrooms. At Stage Right is front door to home leading into small reception hall. Stage Left, past the staircase, is an archway leading to the dining room (which is half visible) and the kitchen beyond (not visible). The furniture is what might be expected—a solid-looking rectangular six-foot sofa flanked by simple, not-too-upholstered armchairs; the usual lamps, end table, coffee table; large secretary-desk against the wall, Left; a circular table surrounded with chairs; a telephone table above the sofa; a reading area by the bay windows. There is a door leading to a small clothes closet under the staircase by the telephone table.*

At Rise: James *sitting at table,* Edith *and* Grace *on sofa. At Curtain,* Harry *is rounding sofa Right and circles sofa, completing his running exercises by* JAMES *at table Left.*

HARRY. 97—98—99—100. O.K., Doc—take my pulse.

GRACE. Well—I wouldn't want to live next door to him. As we came in we just happened to cut across his lawn and I could see those two eyes peeking out the upstairs window at us.

HARRY. (*Defensively.*) The Mayor's a fine fellow.

EDITH. Harry likes the Mayor this year.

JAMES. Yes—I hear he's putting a new four-lane highway right past your lumberyard.

HARRY. Looks pretty good, Doc.

(JAMES *drops* HARRY'S *wrist.*)

JAMES. O.K.

HARRY. Not bad for my age, huh?

JAMES. It's truly remarkable.

(*Voices of* CHARLIE *and* KATE *are heard from upstairs.* HARRY *dons vest and coat which have been draped over chair back.*)

CHARLIE. What time are we supposed to be there?

KATE. Four o'clock. I said we'd come early. (*This reminds* EDITH *of something and she jumps up.*)

EDITH. Oh, dear. (*She starts for the dining room.*)

JAMES. (*Protesting at her departure.*) Edith, where are you going?

EDITH. I have a few things to do—the children are invited out and I—

JAMES. Come on back here. You always have things to do. We came to have a visit. If you don't stay and visit with us I'll claim this is a house call and put it on Harry's bill. (HARRY *is a little worried about this but passes it off as a joke.* EDITH *exits* L.)

HARRY. If everybody was as healthy as I am, you M.D.'s would all be put out of business.

GRACE. Harry—I think that Edith looks—

HARRY. (*Bending his arm.*) Blood pressure of a boy of 21. Look at my teeth.

GRACE. Harry, I think Edith looks a little tired.

HARRY. Don't you worry about Edith. She's like me, made of solid stuff.

(EDITH *re-enters* L. *with her arms full of clothes and starts upstairs.*)

EDITH. Just one moment, Grace.

GRACE. Now, really. Here, Edith, let me help you.

EDITH. No, no, thank you, Grace, I can manage fine. (*She hurries up the stairs and out.*)

JAMES. Harry—Grace is right. Edith does look a little tired.

HARRY. She went to bed early last night. (GRACE *shakes her head over his obtuseness.*)

JAMES. I don't mean tired from lack of a night's sleep. But let's face it, this is a big house to take care of.

HARRY. Why, Edith wouldn't know what to do with herself if she didn't have this house to look after. It's her pride and joy. They don't build houses like this any more, you know. Hardwood floors, best lumber money can buy; granite foundations, copper pipes.

(EDITH *comes downstairs and goes out* L.)

GRACE. Harry, Edith doesn't have a granite foundation or copper pipes.

HARRY. My wife is the healthiest, happiest woman in the whole darn town and I've known that for years.

JAMES. Well, anyhow, Harry, why don't you knock off for a couple of weeks and take Edith on a vacation?

HARRY. A vacation? Just tell me how. We're busier now at the yard than ever. Sure, the help—they can go on a vacation—the boss never gets away.

JAMES. What about your son-in-law?

HARRY. Charlie??

CHARLIE. (*From upstairs.*) Yeah, Dad???

HARRY. Never mind. Do you think I could leave the office for one day and depend on him to look after things? He'd have me ruined in two weeks.

GRACE. Take a one-week vacation.

HARRY. What are you two trying to do to me, anyhow?

JAMES. Oh, come on, Harry! Are you really giving Charlie a fair chance?

HARRY. I've given that son-in-law of mine everything. I gave him a job the day he married Kate. I gave him a nice home here—with me. No expenses. And I also gave him my daughter. Of course, he could complain about that if he had any sense. She's almost as worthless as he is. It's their whole generation, that's what it is. Plain lazy.

(CHARLIE *appears down the stairs, holding a soiled shirt.*)

HARRY. (*Continuing diatribe.*) Won't think for themselves—won't do for themselves.

CHARLIE. Mom—oh, Mom— (*Seeing company.*) Oh, hi!

GRACE. Hello, Charlie.

HARRY. Have to depend on machines thinking and doing for them.

(JAMES *nods.* EDITH *enters from* L. *and looks up at* CHARLIE.)

EDITH. Yes, Charles?

CHARLIE. Kate wants to know if you ironed her blouse.

HARRY. (*It's proving his point.*) See!

EDITH. Oh, it's hanging in the kitchen. I'll get it. (*She starts to go, quickly.*)

CHARLIE. And, Mom—do you do any washing on Sundays?

HARRY. (*Snaps at* CHARLIE.) We're *closed* on Sundays!

CHARLIE. (*Defensively.*) I was only asking.

EDITH. Was it something special, Charles?

CHARLIE. Just this shirt. I wanted to wear it tomorrow, but I don't have to.

EDITH. Give it to me, dear, I have some other things. I'll do it.

CHARLIE. Thanks, Mom.

(CHARLIE *drops shirt over bannister and* EDITH *reaches up to catch it. The shirt floats down, misses* EDITH'S *hands and settles on the floor. She picks it up and exits on way to kitchen as* CHARLIE *goes back into bedroom.*)

HARRY. (*Grumbling to* JAMES.) Gets all his laundry free—all his meals free—no rent to pay. Wouldn't you think he'd show some appreciation?

JAMES. Well, maybe it would be better if he and Kate had their own home.

HARRY. They say they're saving up for one. I don't know how long it will take them—on the money he makes.

(EDITH *rushes into living room carrying blouse and hurries upstairs with it during above dialogue.*)

EDITH. Oh, Kate! Kate, dear? I have your blouse.

(KATE *appears down the stairs wearing a dressing robe. She is a very pretty girl in her late twenties. She takes blouse.*)

KATE. (*Sweetly.*) Thank you, Mother. Oh, and, Mother—would you be a doll and get the fishing boots Charlie borrowed from Jim West?

EDITH. Where are they?

KATE. In the cellar at the bottom of the stairs, I think. It wouldn't be too much trouble, would it?

EDITH. No, no—I'll get them.

(KATE *goes back up into room and* EDITH *rushes downstairs again and exits through dining room.* GRACE *is getting dizzy watching her.*)

GRACE. I'd swear she was on roller-skates—!

JAMES. Harry—are you aware that Edith has been hopping all over this house since we've been here?

HARRY. That's Edith's nature.

GRACE. You mean she's a kangaroo?

JAMES. Grace!

HARRY. Oh, she'll sit down, you'll see. She'll watch her favorite television show later. "Meet the Bride." We can go sit out back till it's over.

JAMES. What do we have to go out back for?

HARRY. I can't stand watching it. It's one of those women's shows. All about newlyweds. A fool announcer throws rice in everybody's face and passes out free honeymoons. A whole half hour of idiots.

JAMES. I've got to go—g'bye, Harry.

HARRY. What's your hurry, Jim?

JAMES. I've got to drop in at the clinic. Grace, I'll pick you up on the way back.

GRACE. O.K., dear.

JAMES. Thanks for the lemonade, Harry.

HARRY. Now, Jim—be careful—don't walk on the Mayor's lawn.

JAMES. Have no fear, Harry. I wouldn't dream of doing anything to jeopardize your new four-lane highway. (*Calls out.*) Good-bye, Edith.

(EDITH *comes running from kitchen carrying pair of hip-length heavy fishing boots.*)

EDITH. Good-bye, James—come again soon.

(JAMES *exits* R., *shuts door.*)

EDITH. Harry? I hate to trouble you, but I think there's something wrong with the hot water boiler.

HARRY. (*As though personally affronted.*) What's that?

EDITH. There's no hot water, dear. I've had the gas turned on, but—

HARRY. That's impossible! You can't buy a better boiler. It's solid copper through and through!

(CHARLIE *appears at top of stairs, razor in hand, towel on shoulder.*)

CHARLIE. What's the matter with the hot water? It's cold.

HARRY. (*Calls up threateningly.*) The hot water in this house isn't cold!

CHARLIE. Well, it isn't hot, either. Do you think there's something wrong with the boiler?

HARRY. There's nothing wrong with the boiler!

EDITH. (*Calls up informatively.*) It just doesn't work, Charles.

HARRY. Now, Edith, please don't insist it doesn't work if you don't know! That boiler was made to last a lifetime.

EDITH. (*Simply.*) Maybe its lifetime is over.

HARRY. Women—! (*Determinedly toward kitchen.*) I'll take a look at it. (*Mumbles to self en route.*) Something wrong with the boiler— Why, it's worked perfectly for twenty-two years! (*He exits.*)

EDITH. Here are your fishing boots, Charles.

CHARLES. Thanks a lot, Mom. I'll get them on my way out. (CHARLES *goes back upstairs.*)

EDITH. I'll put them right down here, dear. (*Puts boots by corner of stair well.*)

GRACE. Now, come on, Edith, for the love of Pete, light somewhere. I want to talk to you.

EDITH. And I want so much to talk to you, Grace. (*Sudden thought.*) Just one little minute.

(EDITH *once more hurries into dining room. Hopelessly frustrated,* GRACE *reaches for her lemonade glass and tosses down the last gulp like a much needed shot of whiskey. A moment later* Edith *returns with an unironed shirt, spectacles and threaded needle in sewing basket. During following conversation she keeps occupied with her mending.*)

Grace. Now what are you going to do?

(Edith *sits down beside* Grace.)

Edith. I don't want to forget this button.

Grace. Honest, it just gives me a pain the way you run around all the time waiting on people.

Edith. Things have to be done, Grace.

Grace. Well—I'm going to give you a piece of advice. And don't tell me to mind my own business.

Edith. Of course I wouldn't. As a matter of fact I was going to ask your advice about—

Grace. Well, here it is. Put your foot down about all this damn housework!

Edith. Well—

Grace. You've just got to get out of that rut—

Edith. Oh, Grace—I—

Grace. It's easy. Just go out to dinner a couple of times a week. Harry can afford it.

Edith. It isn't that. But Harry works all day and at night he likes to come home and have a good dinner and relax. He just loves my cooking. He still comes home for lunch. I guess that proves something.

Grace. It sure does. And I won't mention what. Have you ever thought about getting a maid?

Edith. Harry's always had a feeling against maids. He says, here you are in your own home, and there's no privacy.

Grace. Have you ever thought of making him take you out? Go to the movies once in a while.

Edith. Well, Harry says— (*Suddenly the sound of CLANKING emanates from direction of kitchen caused by furious rapping of hammer against pipes.* Edith *and*

GRACE *are startled, they look at each other.* EDITH *rises quickly.*) I wonder what he's doing in there?

GRACE. (*Restrains* EDITH.) Edith!—Edith, don't worry about him. He's having a wonderful time banging away at his solid copper lifetime boiler. Besides, it gives us a chance to talk.

EDITH. My goodness, how we used to talk once, didn't we though?

GRACE. Yes. And I gave you a lot of good advice—you ignored about ninety percent of it—but here I am trying again.

EDITH. I love you, Grace.

GRACE. We're a couple of middle-aged women and I know we're not supposed to behave like kids, but there's no law that says we can't have any fun.

EDITH. Oh—I do—I do—

GRACE. Let me finish. I mean frivolous fun! You know—

EDITH. (*Leans forward. Urgently.*) Grace, there's something I've simply got to force myself to tell you. Actually I should talk to James about it, I guess. But— (CHARLIE *appears at top of stairs, fully dressed.*) I'll have to tell you later—!

(*SOUND emanates from direction of kitchen.*)

CHARLIE. What's all the noise?

EDITH. It's Harry. Trying to get the water hot.

CHARLIE. By rubbing the pipes together? Why doesn't he call a plumber?

(KATE *now appears at top of stairs, looking crisp and lovely. She descends, a smile of greeting on her pretty face.*)

EDITH. (*To* CHARLIE.) You know what Harry says about plumbers!

CHARLIE. Yeah, like throwing money down the drain.

KATE. (*Extending hand.*) Hello, Grace.
GRACE. Hello, Kate dear.
EDITH. Are you children coming home for dinner?
KATE. No, Mother.
CHARLIE. I'd just as soon.
KATE. (*Meaningfully.*) And I'd just as soon *eat out.* I'm in the mood for dinner and dancing!

(HARRY *barges in, carrying a wrench and a hammer, his face smudged and his shirt soiled.*)

HARRY. (*Bellowing.*) What happened to my blow torch???
EDITH. (*Startled.*) Doesn't that work, either?
HARRY. Of *course* it works. You couldn't buy a better blow torch. I want to know where it *is,* that's what I want to know!
CHARLIE. Are you going to try to heat the water with a *blow torch?*
HARRY. (*Somehow his son-in-law rubs him the wrong way.*) It wouldn't hurt, you know, if you came in to see if I needed any help!
CHARLIE. Gee, Dad, I don't know anything about hot water boilers!
HARRY. Well, neither do I! But that doesn't stop me from *fixing* it.
KATE. Well—did you get it fixed?
HARRY. Yes! I just can't get the pipes and things back together.
EDITH. I'm sure Charles would be more than glad to help you, dear, but he and Kate have a social engagement.
HARRY. Again? (*To* KATE *and* CHARLIE.) Don't you two ever stay home?
KATE. (*Used to her father's blustering.*) We're home all week.
HARRY. *I* never see you. I haven't seen you at the breakfast table in five years.

KATE. (*Simply.*) I don't eat breakfast. Is there any sense in getting up for breakfast if I don't eat any?

EDITH. (*To her daughter's defense.*) Kate eats lunch.

HARRY. What you *mean* is—she eats breakfast, but doesn't get up until it's *time* for lunch!

CHARLIE. You can't say you don't see *me* all week.

HARRY. Don't remind me! Know what you two need? *Responsibility*. It's time you settled down and started raising a family!

KATE. Now, Father—we're not going to start raising a family right here in the middle of the living room. Please let's not go into that again.

CHARLIE. Besides—we're not ready yet.

HARRY. What's it take to get ready? Huh? It's *time* you were ready. All you have to do is make up your mind and sit down and do it!

KATE. Father—!

CHARLIE. It's a little embarrassing, you know. Just because you can't find your blow torch.

EDITH. (*Nicely.*) Why don't you go look for your blow torch, dear? You'll feel better if you find it.

KATE. Besides, we have to leave. (*Crosses to* GRACE.) I'm sorry we missed Doctor Jim.

GRACE. Just enjoy yourselves.

CHARLIE. (*To* GRACE.) I'll come up to his office one of these days. For some time now I've had a little lump on the back of my head—

HARRY. It figures—

(CHARLIE *and* HARRY *exchange sharp glances.*)

GRACE. I'll tell him, Charlie.

KATE. (*Kisses* EDITH.) 'Bye, Mother.

EDITH. Have a nice day, dear.

KATE. (*Gives* HARRY *a kiss.*) 'Bye, Father.

CHARLIE. (*Kisses* EDITH.) S'long, Mom.

EDITH. Now, drive carefully. You know Sunday traffic.

CHARLIE. I will. (*Crosses to door. Turns awkwardly to*

HARRY.) Well—uh—see you later, Dad.

(HARRY *grunts something unintelligible.* CHARLIE *and* KATE *cross to front door and wave last good-bye.*)

KATE. We'll try not to be too late. (*And they exit.*)

HARRY. (*Crosses to door, then* D.C. *Finally; shaking head.*) There's just no home life any more. Everybody's in a rush to go somewhere. No roots.

GRACE. Times change, Harry. There's a big world out there.

HARRY. (*Crosses toward dining room.*) And who needs it!

EDITH. You can't tie young people down, dear.

HARRY. I'm not trying to tie them down! I want them to tie *themselves* down.

GRACE. The important thing is that they seem happy.

EDITH. And that's what counts, Harry.

HARRY. They're happy because they've got *me,* that's why they're happy! (*Pokes own chest with rigid thumb.*) I *make* them happy!

EDITH. It's true, dear—you do cause a lot of happiness.

HARRY. You're darn right! Now I'd better find that blow torch. (*He exits.*)

GRACE. (*After watching him go.*) You know, Edith—He really believes every word he says—!

EDITH. That's one thing about Harry. He doesn't lie. He's as honest as the day is long.

GRACE. (*Half to self.*) What long days they must be—(*But* EDITH *doesn't hear for at the same moment she spies the fishing boots at the bottom of the stair well.*)

EDITH. Oh, dear! Charles completely forgot the fishing boots!

(*She rushes to them, grabs them up and starts running toward the front door. But halfway she suddenly stops, falters, drops the boots and presses a hand to her breast as she reaches for support.* GRACE *is sud-*

denly aware. With immediate concern GRACE *rushes to her side and helps support her.*)

GRACE. Edith! What is it???

EDITH. (*Dizzily.*) It's— It's what I started to tell you, Grace—and why I want to see James at his office. . . .

(GRACE *observes* EDITH *with great concern.*)

CURTAIN

ACT ONE

SCENE 2

TIME: *The next day. The time is six-thirty in the evening.*

AT RISE: KATE *is sitting on a chair, looking at a chic woman's magazine;* CHARLIE *is sitting on divan, hunched over coffee table engrossed in game of solitaire;* HARRY *is pacing nervously.* HARRY *stops pacing long enough to check the time on his watch, then throws up his hands and continues pacing.*

HARRY. Where was she going?

KATE. I don't know, Father.

HARRY. But you said you dropped her off.

KATE. Yes, I did, but—

HARRY. How could you drop her off without knowing where she was going?

KATE. Mother's a big girl now, I thought it was safe to let her out alone.

HARRY. You watch your manners.

CHARLIE. (*Off on his own.*) What I wouldn't give for a red jack—

(KATE *affords* CHARLIE *a quick, disgusted look.*)

KATE. There's one in the desk drawer.

(HARRY *confronts* KATE *as* KATE *tries to go back to her magazine.*)

HARRY. Don't you think it's a little unusual for your mother to be away from home this late? It's after six-thirty!

CHARLIE. (*As he continues, engrossed in game.*) And we haven't eaten since lunch.

HARRY. This is serious! Do you realize we don't know where she is? The table hasn't been set—there's no sign of dinner— It's like one of those ghost ships you read about. Everything's in order except the crew's missing!

CHARLIE. Yeah—I read a story like that once.

KATE. Well, this is no ghost ship and mother is not a *crew*.

CHARLIE. (*To* KATE.) Where'd you say that red jack was?

KATE. Are you *kidding—?*

HARRY. (*He turns violently on* CHARLIE.) Is that all you can do is sit there playing that game!

CHARLIE. (*He reacts with a start; then, defensively.*) What's wrong in a little solitaire? It's just *cards*.

HARRY. You know I don't tolerate any gambling in this house!

(*With a long-suffering look, and knowing what is to come,* KATE *goes back to her magazine.*)

CHARLIE. Who's gambling?

HARRY. Don't ask *me* "who's gambling"! Anybody who plays cards *gambles*. (*Furthering his point.*) Somebody has to win and somebody has to lose, don't they?

CHARLIE. But I'm the only one playing.

HARRY. (*Bitingly.*) Are you winning?

CHARLIE. I can't find a red jack.

HARRY. Then you're losing, *right?*

CHARLIE. (*Draws self up with dignity.*) I don't have

to answer that! I'm not finished yet. I don't give up that easily, you know.

HARRY. (*He bends close to* CHARLIE, *his eyes narrowing challengingly.*) That's the way all gamblers talk once they're *hooked*.

CHARLIE. Who says I'm hooked? I don't even *like* to gamble.

HARRY. And alcoholics don't like liquor either, but they still can't resist it!

CHARLIE. (*Indignantly.*) Now, wa——it a minute! There's nothing alcoholic about my playing a little solitaire. I can give it up like— (*Snaps fingers.*) *that*.

HARRY. All right. Let me see you give it up right now. Go ahead.

CHARLIE. Think I can't do it?

HARRY. I'm waiting. Go ahead.

CHARLIE. (*He is about to boldly sweep the cards away, but just can't bring himself to do it.*) Why should I! If I could find a red jack I could play out.

HARRY. (*Sneeringly.*) See? I told you you were hooked.

KATE. (*From behind magazine.*) Charlie—why don't you admit you're hooked? Believe me, it would be much easier.

CHARLIE. I don't have to admit anything that isn't true. (*To* HARRY.) Just because Mom isn't home you want to take it out on me.

HARRY. Doesn't it bother you that she's out there someplace and we don't know where?

CHARLIE. Then why don't we call the police?

HARRY. Boy—! *that's* a bright idea. And what makes you think she's mixed up with the police?

CHARLIE. I didn't say she was mixed up with the police. I just thought that if she's lost, maybe the police could find her.

HARRY. And you'd like to see it in the newspaper and everything, huh!

CHARLIE. Who said I wanted it to get in the newspaper? I don't even know what she's done.

KATE. (*Unable to remain silent any longer.*) Will you

two please stop all this nonsense? If you could hear yourselves, you wouldn't believe it.

HARRY. (*Snapping at* KATE.) You seem to be calm enough about it all. Have you ever known your mother to be away from home this late before?

KATE. I refuse to get panicky. If anything serious had happened we would have heard.

CHARLIE. Yeah. Mom has identification, hasn't she?

HARRY. She has a birthmark.

CHARLIE. (*Absorbed in cards.*) Is her address on it?

HARRY. Who the hell ever heard of an address on a *birthmark?*

CHARLIE. (*Realizes.*) I was thinking of something else.

HARRY. You're an idiot!

CHARLIE. (*He stands up squarely.*) I take exception to that!

HARRY. (*He advances one precise step toward* CHARLIE, *ready to take up the challenge.*) Is this the showdown?

CHARLIE. You'd like it to be, wouldn't you!

KATE. (*Rises, throws magazine on sofa.*) You two are going to make me scream—I swear! If you don't stop—(*And then, as the* TWO MEN *stand squared off at each other, the front door opens and closes. All eyes focus on* EDITH *as she enters living room. We can hardly recognize* EDITH, *for she is a completely changed person. Her hair is cut short, her application of makeup does wonders for her, the silly little hat atop her head gives her that certain touch, and her whole demeanor has changed.* EDITH *stops, poses for inspection. All mouths are agape and speechless. Finally.*) Mother—!

CHARLIE. Mom—!

(*But* HARRY *remains paralyzed.*)

EDITH. (*Almost singing with joy.*) Do you like it?

HARRY. What have you done to yourself???

EDITH. For heaven's sake! Is that all anybody has to say?

HARRY. (*Finally pulls self together.*) What's that thing on top of your head? Have you forgotten you have a family! Where've you been?

EDITH. Well—I spent most of the afternoon with Grace. She just dropped me off.

HARRY. *Where's dinner?*

EDITH. (*Hand goes delicately to new hat.*) Oh, I'm sorry, but in all the excitement— Well, I guess I'm wearing it. I spent the meat money for it. Is it late?

(KATE, HARRY *and* CHARLIE *exchange worried glances.* KATE *takes the initiative.*)

KATE. Mother—why don't you sit down and we'll talk?

EDITH. Fine—I certainly have a lot to tell you. All of you. (EDITH *sits down, pulls a large pin from her hat, removes it and tosses her head freely.*)

HARRY. (*Aghast.*) Where's your hair?!

EDITH. (*She pats her head vainly, trying to conceal disappointment.*) Harry Lambert! If that isn't the silliest—

HARRY. But it's gone. I can see!

EDITH. No—no—it's just shorter, that's all. Shorter and curled at the ends. I had a permanent, and a facial, and a manicure—the girl said they gave me the works.

HARRY. They gave you *what?*

KATE. I think you look just lovely, Mother.

CHARLIE. Chee!!! Some difference.

EDITH. It cost twenty-five dollars.

HARRY. Edith, you go right back down there and get your money back!

EDITH. That isn't a nice way to talk. Especially—when I tell you what I'm going to tell you.

Now HARRY. Edith, you just sit there. quietly I'm going to make a little call to the doctor. Now don't excite yourself. He's very good.

EDITH. But, Harry—you don't have to call him. I just came from his office. That's what I want to tell you about.

(EVERYBODY *looks at her even more puzzledly.*)

HARRY. You *were* at the Doctor's office?

(EDITH *nods reassuringly.*)

KATE. Well, what *for,* Mother?

EDITH. Harry, Kate—and you too, Charles. I want you to sit down. Go ahead.

(HARRY *and* CHARLIE *rush for same chair;* CHARLIE *wins;* HARRY *rushes around sofa to other chair. They sit, keeping their bewildered eyes fixed on* EDITH.)

HARRY. (*Gently, so as not to disturb her obvious border-line sanity.*) Now, tell us. We're all sitting down nicely.

(EDITH *hesitates.* KATE *pats her comfortingly.*)

KATE. It's all right, Mother. We're all listening. (*To* HARRY *and* CHARLIE *with a nod.*) Aren't we?

(HARRY *and* CHARLIE *nod back.*)

CHARLIE. I'm listening. (*Observes* EDITH *again.*)

KATE. We're your family and we love you.

EDITH. (*Smiles warmly into each face.*) I was counting on that. (*Relaxes with a deep, comforting sigh.*) Well, I guess I should start from the *very beginning.*

KATE. Start anywhere you want, Mother.

EDITH. Or maybe not from the *very* beginning. Perhaps the middle.

HARRY. All right, start from the middle. But *start.*

CHARLIE. I'd like to hear it from the beginning.

HARRY. (*Turning on* CHARLIE.) If you don't know

what she's talking about, how do you know you'd like to hear it from the beginning!

CHARLIE. I just thought—

KATE. Would you both mind letting *Mother* talk? (*To* EDITH.) Then start from the middle, Mother.

EDITH. (*Losing courage.*) I'd really rather start from the end and get it over with, but—

HARRY. Then tell us the *end*.

EDITH. No, I'll start from yesterday. (HARRY *goes limp.*) After all, yesterday was really the beginning if you want to look at it that way.

HARRY. (*Beseechingly.*) We'll look at it any way you want, Edith.

KATE. Then start from yesterday, Mother. Just start.

CHARLIE. (*Trying to be helpful.*) Would you rather have us try and guess? Maybe if you just gave us a *hint*.

HARRY. (*He turns furiously on* CHARLIE.) We're not playing *parlor* games! We're trying to get some information!

CHARLIE. Well, we're not getting any information *this* way. I think it's a pretty *good* suggestion, if it will help.

HARRY. Just like all the rest of your suggestions! If I listened to your suggestions down at the lumberyard, I'd have been broke the first year you were here!

CHARLIE. That happens to be one man's *opinion*.

HARRY. Are you trying to tell me I don't know my own business!

KATE. Will you please stop it!

EDITH. (*Nobody's paying any attention to her now. Sits up straight with hands folded in lap.*) I'm going to have a baby.

(*But her announcement is lost in the flare-up between* HARRY, CHARLIE *and* KATE.)

HARRY. (*To* KATE.) I won't stop what I didn't *start*. (*At* CHARLIE.) Now *answer* me. Are you trying to tell me I don't know my own business?

CHARLIE. I didn't say that. But other people can be right once in a while, too, you know!

HARRY. (*A big HUH!*) *You,* for instance?

EDITH. I'm going to have a *baby.*

KATE. (*Snapping at* HARRY *and* CHARLIE.) Would you *mind* letting Mother say what she's got to say?

HARRY. Now, you stay out of this. You're not taking Charlie's side again. We're going to have this out— (*But suddenly* EDITH'S *words register. There is a dead silence as all* THREE *look at* EDITH.) W-we—didn't quite hear you, Edith.

KATE. (*Cautiously.*) D-did you say something, Mother?

CHARLIE. I—I think I heard her—

EDITH. (*Announces once more; exactly and proudly.*) I said—I'm going to have a *baby.* There.

(HARRY *flops into chair;* KATE *draws back almost in terror; and* CHARLIE *just gapes.*)

KATE. Mother!!!

CHARLIE. Chee!

EDITH. (*Smiling happily.*) Now you know.

KATE. (*She breaks out in an anguished cry.*) Father—*how could* you!

HARRY. (*He draws himself up with dignity.*) Now look here! Look here—!

(CHARLIE *goes to* KATE'S *side, putting his arm on her shoulder as* KATE *continues sobbing in a handkerchief.*)

CHARLIE. (*Stalwartly to* HARRY.) And *I* think that's a pretty underhanded trick!

HARRY. (*He is cornered, his jowls quivering. Rises.*) Trick? *Trick?*

CHARLIE. Yeah. You've been throwing everything else in my face, now I suppose it'll be the baby.

HARRY. (*For lack of any other defense.*) Now, look here!

EDITH. (*Consolingly, to* CHARLIE.) Now, now—nobody's going to throw the baby in your face. (*To* HARRY.) And I want you to promise Charles that.

HARRY. I don't have to promise him anything! Something is out of control here and I'm going to get to the bottom of this! (*Looks firmly at* EDITH.)

EDITH. (*Mild warning.*) Now, Harry—you're raising your voice. And that is the sort of thing that is likely to make me faint, you know— (*She sinks onto sofa. This has its desired effect.* HARRY *straightens, looks incredulously at his wife.*)

HARRY. *You—faint?*

KATE. (*Through her tears.*) You seem to forget what condition Mother is in. (*Buries her head in* EDITH'S *shoulder.*) Oh, *Mother!*

(EDITH *pats the top of* KATE'S *miserable head.*)

EDITH. There, there, dear— Remember how you always said you wanted a little brother— (*This only makes* KATE *sob harder.*)

KATE. That was twenty years ago!

EDITH. (*Contentedly.*) Your wish has finally come true.

HARRY. (*Frantically.*) The hell with *her* wishes! What about *mine?*

EDITH. Now, Harry—you have to realize the first consideration must be for the children. Don't forget Kate is an only child, and it's going to be a delicate situation bringing another child into the family. (HARRY *clamps his hands to his face, trying to keep his sanity.* EDITH *looks compassionately at her weeping daughter.*) Kate, dear—if it's a little brother, promise me now that you'll get along together.

KATE. Mother, I'm not going to crawl into his crib and start a fight with him. (*Just can't reconcile herself.*) But how will I ever introduce him to my friends!

CHARLIE. (*He puts hand on* KATE'S *shoulder consolingly.*) Honey— Don't cry.

KATE. (*Rises, runs across to table.*) Don't you touch me! (CHARLIE *withdraws hand as though he had touched hot stove.*) All men are *horrible!*

CHARLIE. Kate, I had nothing to do with this.

HARRY. (*To* CHARLIE.) Have you any idea what you're talking about! (*Then to* KATE.) And you stop crying. If anybody should *cry* around here it should be me!

EDITH. I thought everyone would be so happy—

HARRY. Well—we are happy, Edith. But there's all kinds of happiness. This happens to be the kind of happiness that—that—well, everybody isn't happy about! (*Sits.*)

EDITH. (*So lovingly.*) But, Harry!—a little *baby*— (*At the very mention,* KATE'S *well of tears flows anew.*)

CHARLIE. Would it be all right if I smoked?

HARRY. (*At* CHARLIE.) Haven't you an ounce of *respect?*

KATE. How could you even *think* of smoking at a time like this?

CHARLIE. It's only a cigarette! I'm not gonna blow the house up!

EDITH. You go ahead and smoke, Charles. Now there's no reason why we can't continue leading normal lives. And that goes for you, Kate—and you too, Harry. In fact Grace thinks I should live even more fully.

HARRY. (*He almost breaks down and whimpers.*) Normal lives— Edith, is there the slightest chance you made a mistake? That there was some other woman in the doctor's office he might have been talking about? A *young* woman—with a *nice young husband?*

EDITH. (*A little confused now.*) But James said—

KATE. Father—why don't you call the doctor and find out *exactly.*

HARRY. (*Determinedly.*) That's a good idea! (*He goes to phone—dials.*)

EDITH. Now, Harry—you mustn't be cross with James.

I know he couldn't have made a mistake because I was sure before I even went to him. Don't forget, Harry—you're not a woman.

HARRY. (*Finds number and dials.*) I won't forget!

KATE. Now try and speak *plainly,* Father.

HARRY. Uh, hello—*Jim?* This is Harry Lambert— (*He is interrupted, becomes rigid, repeats aloud.*) Congratulations—? Now look, Jim—you must understand that—(*Listens; nods twice. Listens with a more sickly expression.*) Oh, sure—I know about those things. (*Listens.*) Believe me—you don't have to worry about her. (*Nods.*) We have some in the medicine cabinet. I'll take them whenever I need them. Don't worry—I won't be sick for a while. (*Listens; nods.*) All right—I'll tell her. 'Bye. (*Hangs up receiver and just stands there a few seconds, then crosses* D. C., *sits.*)

EDITH. (*Brightly.*) Well?

CHARLIE. It's true—huh?

KATE. There's no doubt about it?

HARRY. (*He nods.*) Your mother is going to have a baby, and—so am I.

EDITH. (*Couldn't be more pleased.*) *There!*

CHARLIE. Well, I guess congratulations are in order. (*Smiles feebly and makes a general motion with his hand.*) Congratulations.

KATE. (*Trying to smile sweetly at* EDITH.) Congratulations!

HARRY. Congratulations, Edith.

EDITH. (*Touched.*) And congratulations to you, Harry.

HARRY. Thank you. (*Sinks down in a chair.*) Of course you must realize this is somewhat of a shock to me. I haven't prepared myself for this exactly. It is a little unusual, you know—

EDITH. That's what I told James. But he said it does happen at our age, much more often than people realize.

CHARLIE. Yeah—I remember reading someplace—

HARRY. This is *past* the reading stage! (*Gets to his feet and starts pacing.*) What have I done? I've led a good life. I've worked hard. Don't smoke much. Don't drink or gamble.

CHARLIE. That's true, Dad. You have very few vices. As a matter of fact—I didn't even think you— (*Thinks twice.*)

EDITH. And you know something, Harry dear? Because of that, you're as healthy today as you were twenty years ago.

HARRY. Please—don't remind me of it!

KATE. I think we're all a little overwrought.

EDITH. Oh, no. I feel fine. As a matter of fact, I'm hungry. Oh, dear—and I haven't even started dinner, yet.

CHARLIE. Yeah—I'm hungry, too.

EDITH. I'll hurry.

(*But* HARRY *snaps out of his present state of self-pity, raising a restraining hand to* EDITH *as he rises.*)

HARRY. Oh, no, you don't, Edith. According to Jim you're supposed to take things easier. No standing on your feet over a hot stove. Having a baby is nothing to laugh about. And we're all in this thing together. (*Turns militarily to* KATE.) Kate—we're hungry!

KATE. (*She reacts almost with terror, her whole immediate future dawning upon her like an ominous shadow.*) But—I can't cook!

EDITH. (*Dismissing the whole idea.*) Harry—it's no chore for me to get the dinner—

HARRY. (*But he stands firm.*) A change has to be made, Edith, and there's no time like the present.

KATE. (*Bravely.*) Then I think there's something else we ought to discuss.

HARRY. (*He casts a suspicious glance at his daughter.*) And what's that?

KATE. (*Realizing possible consequences.*) A maid.

(EVERYBODY *looks to* HARRY *for his reaction, and get just what they expected.*)

HARRY. A *WHAT?*

(EVERYBODY *cringes at expected reaction.*)

KATE. Well, mother won't be able to do any real work, so—

HARRY. So you'll do it! And I'd say it was about time! You've never lifted a *finger* in this house. And I won't have any maids sneaking around here!

KATE. (*Lifts her chin high; courageously.*) All right—I'll do it! I'll do *everything*. I'll become a *slave! That's* what you want!

HARRY. (*Jerks head with acceptance.*) That's more like it!

KATE. (*Then she faces everyone squarely and stoically announces:*) I will call when dinner is ready—*whatever* it is. (*With this, she turns militarily and exits through dining room.* CHARLIE *looks bewilderedly from his wife to* HARRY *and* EDITH.)

CHARLIE. Maybe I'd better go in and help her. (*Apologetically.*) Her first time and all—

(CHARLIE *exits in* KATE'S *trail. There is an empty silence, then* HARRY *stares blankly off into space.* EDITH *observes him tenderly.*)

EDITH. (*Softly.*) Harry—? (*He does not respond.*) Harry, dear—?

HARRY. (*Still staring off blankly.*) Yes?

EDITH. It was very thoughtful of you not wanting me to stand on my feet—and to cook dinner over a hot stove. Did you do it just because James advised it? I mean—would you have thought of it *anyhow?*

HARRY. Those were Jim's orders. He knows best.

EDITH. (*She hides her disappointment with an ever-so-slight smile, sits down near him.*) Don't be upset, Harry—this should really be a joyous occasion.

HARRY. (*Sits.*) Oh, I'm joyous— It's just that I'm so—so miserable.

EDITH. You know, dear—if you look at it right, this is a fine and noble thing we're doing. We're giving life to a brand-new little human being. A baby. Isn't that beautiful? (*Coaxes him gently.*) Why don't you try to look at it that way, dear? Try—

HARRY. (*Swallows.*) I'm trying—

EDITH. Can you see it that way now?

HARRY. I'm still trying.

EDITH. (*She considers, tries another approach.*) Well, then, look at it this way. You've always wanted a son and now you might have one. Isn't that a nice thought?

HARRY. Edith, the one thought that keeps going through my mind is that when he gets out of college, I'll be going on eighty-three, if he's *smart*—

EDITH. Of course he'll be smart, dear. Your son? Why, he'll take after you. He'll have your nice eyes—your brains—the curly hair you used to have. (*Drifts off into thought.*) It makes one believe in miracles. . . . Don't you think it makes one believe in miracles, Harry? You'd never have thought it possible, would you?

HARRY. (*Rises, crosses* D. R.) You can be sure of that, Edith.

EDITH. And yet it's true. Harry, how does that poem go?

HARRY. I shot an arrow into the air—?

EDITH. No, Harry. No—not that one.

HARRY. It's the only one I can think of.

EDITH. I guess it doesn't matter. (*They both fall silent again. Then:*) Harry—?

HARRY. Yes—

EDITH. You're not angry with me, are you? Because of —this?

HARRY. No—

EDITH. Am I foolish in thinking it's sort of romantic? Even at our age? I'm sorry about the hat. I guess it was silly of me, but—I don't know. When James told me the news, for a while there I just felt young again. I can take the hat back if you want me to, Harry.

HARRY. Keep it.

EDITH. Then you like it?

HARRY. (*Turns head to look, slowly turns front.*) Keep it, anyway.

EDITH. You know, Harry—the girls at the beauty parlor were so nice to me when I told them I was going to have a baby. They joked good-naturedly with me—everything. There was this young blond girl—the manicurist—she was so funny. D'you know what she said, Harry?

HARRY. What did she say?

EDITH. (*Tries to repress little laugh.*) She said— You won't be embarrassed if I repreat it, will you?

HARRY. Why, was it about me?

EDITH. Well, it wasn't *really* about you. It was just a little joke, that's all. It was meant in the nicest way.

HARRY. What did she say?

EDITH. Well—just so you don't take it wrong, I want you to promise that you'll imagine yourself sitting in the beauty parlor under the dryer with all these cheerful women around and this pretty, young blond girl.

HARRY. Edith, I refuse to imagine myself in a beauty parlor!

EDITH. Well, it came out of just woman talk. You know. I mean it was harmless. Well, anyway—at one part of the conversation this young manicurist just sort of whistled and she shook her head and she said— Are you listening, Harry?

HARRY. She sort of whistled and shook her head and said—

EDITH. Well, she said: "Sister"—she meant me—"Sister," she said, "there must be life in the ole boy yet!" (*There is a long pause. She puts her hand on his knee; he brushes it off.*) Harry, you've *got* to imagine yourself in the beauty parlor. Why, these women were laughing *with* you. It was really a *compliment*. I felt sort of proud of you, even though it was said lightly. Don't you understand, Harry?

(*Another pause as* EDITH *prays* HARRY *will share her sentiment.*)

HARRY. Perfectly!

EDITH. (*With relief.*) It's going to be so wonderful having an innocent little child in the house. (*In a world of her own now.*) I was thinking. You know that extra bedroom next to ours? The one we never use? It will be ideal for the nursery! We're going to *need* a nursery, you know.

HARRY. (*From the lower depths.*) I suppose—

EDITH. Then can I fix it up? The wallpaper in there is just terrible. Is it all right if I get new wallpaper?

HARRY. If you want to, Edith—

EDITH. Oh, Harry—you're so sweet! Of course, I don't know how much it's going to cost.

HARRY. Get the best paper money can buy. Whatever it comes to, just make out a check for it.

EDITH. A check?

HARRY. A check.

EDITH. (*Reflecting.*) Do you know, I had completely forgotten about that? I've just been living for years off the food allowance you give me. That's right—I *can* write out a check, can't I?

HARRY. You always could. We've always had a joint account.

EDITH. I don't believe I even know where my check book *is*—

HARRY. It's in the desk over there. In the locked compartment.

EDITH. (*She becomes excited over prospect.*) Do I have a key?

HARRY. I don't remember.

EDITH. Harry, let me have yours! I want to see my check book.

HARRY. (*He produces his key ring and selects key for her.*) Here.

(EDITH *takes key and rushes to desk. Opening the compartment she extracts several bank books.* EDITH *shuffles through the books.* CHARLIE *enters wearing dish towel around waist.*)

CHARLIE. Hey, Mom, where's the can opener? I looked in the drawer.

EDITH. On the shelf—above the stove, Charles.

CHARLIE. Thanks, Mom. (*Exits.*)

EDITH. Harry—? Which one of these bank books is the good one?

HARRY. *Which* one? They're *all* good.

EDITH. (*She thumbs through the books, making quick mental calculations.*) You mean that—? Harry—I didn't know we had *this* much money! Why there's a *fortune* here!

HARRY. There's nothing of the sort.

EDITH. (*Crosses to sofa.*) There most certainly *is.* (*Then sudden thought.*) Do you know that I've been squeezing your oranges by hand for thirty years? I could have bought an electric squeezer—

HARRY. (*Weakly.*) Edith, please— Let's not go into squeezing oranges now. I don't care if I never see another orange— (*Starts wearily toward stairs.*) Now don't forget what Jim said. Plenty of rest. And—and don't you worry about a thing. (*Thinks.*) I'll worry. (*He slowly starts up the stairs.*)

EDITH. Are you going upstairs, dear? (HARRY *nods.*) I'll come with you. I'd like to freshen up before dinner.

(EDITH *crosses to foot of stairs. After* HARRY *is halfway up the stairs he stops, slowly turns, and look down at* EDITH, *who has just started up.* EDITH *also stops, looks up at* HARRY, *for a moment they both just stand there. Then, self-consciously,* HARRY *comes back down, gently cups a helping hand to* EDITH'S *elbow and escorts her up.* EDITH *holds her head regally and swallows back the lump in her throat as they continue on together during lowering of:*)

CURTAIN

ACT TWO

SCENE 1

TIME: *Almost six o'clock in the evening, a few days later.*

We hear sound of HAMMERING and SAWING emanating from upstairs. MR. FOLEY, *a long, thin man wearing carpenter's garb, is showing* EDITH *a large blueprint.*

FOLEY. —An' y'see right here in the 'riginal blueprints o' the house? Well, f'the new bathroom we're gonna have t'extend the plumbing which means rippin' up the whole floor. Awright?

EDITH. If you have to, you have to, Mr. Foley. A bathroom just wouldn't be a bathroom without plumbing.

FOLEY. That's a very good point. 'Course it'll be an added expense.

EDITH. Oh, that's quite all right, Mr. Foley. I can sign checks, you know.

FOLEY. Well, then with your okay, I'll jus' go right ahead. Be here again with my men firs' thing in the morning. (*Looks at pocket watch, then goes to foot of stairs. He cups hand to mouth and calls up piercingly.*) Quittin' time! (*Hammering and sawing stops instantly.* FOLEY *crosses to table.*)

EDITH. My! They certainly obey your orders, don't they?

FOLEY. They're certain things they understand better'n others.

HARRY'S VOICE. (*Heard roaring Off* R.) Edith! Charlie—get hold of that thing, will ya'!

FOLEY. (*Looking out.*) Well, Mr. Lambert's come home, I see.

HARRY'S VOICE. You heard me—get hold of it!

FOLEY. (*Yells upstairs.*) Oscar!

OSCAR'S VOICE. Yoo.

FOLEY. Down the back stairs, boys.

OSCAR'S VOICE. Right.

FOLEY. (*Calling upstairs as he goes.*) Meet you at the car. (*He exits* L.)

HARRY'S VOICE. (*Off* R.) Certainly, pick it up! Get it out of sight.

(HARRY *enters in a state of emotional panic.*)

HARRY. Edith, what's going on around here! What are those things doing out there?

EDITH. But, Harry—if you let me—

HARRY. (*Turns and calls off* R.) Bring it in here, I said.

EDITH. But, Harry, if you'll let me—

(CHARLIE *enters carrying porcelain toilet commode.*)

CHARLIE. What do you want me to do with it?

HARRY. Put it anywhere. Drop it. Break it. Come out here and help me with this other. (*He rushes out and we hear his* VOICE *Offstage calling.*) Charlie!

CHARLIE. (*Putting down the commode below table,* D. C.) I'm coming. (*Hurries out* R.)

EDITH. (*Going to the door.*) Oh, dear! (*As they enter carrying a porcelain tub.*) Harry, it's all very simple, I—

HARRY. (*To* CHARLIE *who precedes him.*) Be careful! Out there on the lawn! What'll people think??

EDITH. Mind the chair! Don't drop it!

CHARLIE. This is heavy.

HARRY. I know it's heavy!

(*They set the tub down between the sofa and the desk.*)

EDITH. Now, Harry—if you'll just calm down, I'll tell you—

HARRY. (*Furiously.*) Don't tell me a thing! Just answer my questions. (*Shoots accusing finger at tub and com-

mode.) What's that, and what's that? And what's all that lumber outside? I'm asking for "what's," Edith, and I want them!

EDITH. That's a new bathtub, Harry, and you know what *that* is.

HARRY. Of course I know what that is, and so do all our neighbors! What are they doing sitting out there in the driveway??

EDITH. That's where they were unloaded, dear. They weren't going to leave them there. It's for the new bathroom.

HARRY. What new bathroom?

EDITH. For the nursery. Now, if you'll just listen, I'll tell you all the details.

HARRY. I don't want the details. I just want the facts. (*Stops. Watches* CHARLIE *who is kneeling by commode examining it.*) What are you doing?

CHARLIE. This is very interesting. You know what the name of this thing is?

HARRY. I think I am going out of my mind.

EDITH. You're just excited, dear.

CHARLIE. Sure! Look, it's called a Crane. See—there's the name on it right there. Maybe that's where Mayor Crane's family got their dough. I bet there's good money in those things. You know that—

HARRY. Will you shut up?

EDITH. Now, Harry, you're just being stubborn. All this is going to be a great improvement.

CHARLIE. Sure. That's the kind I've always wanted. The one upstairs—

HARRY. (*He glares at* CHARLIE.) Do you mind if we get back on the original subject!

CHARLIE. Look, Dad—if you don't want me around, just *say* so.

HARRY. All right! I don't want you around!!

EDITH. (*Admonishingly.*) *Harry!*

CHARLIE. (*But he intends to rise above his father-in-law's vulgarity.*) It's all right, Mom. Where's Kate?

EDITH. She's in the kitchen—fixing a roast for dinner.

HARRY. Why don't you go in and roast with her!

CHARLIE. (*He looks at* HARRY *as though the latter was beyond hope.*) Chee—! (*He exits through dining room.*)

EDITH. You know, Harry—you're entirely too cross with Charles. Nothing he does is right.

HARRY. *You're* telling *me!*

EDITH. I didn't mean it that way. I meant—everything he does is wrong.

HARRY. I know what you mean, Edith, but don't let me get upset over Charlie, let me get upset over *you.*

EDITH. Well, there's nothing to get upset about, so why don't you sit down and relax. Relax, dear. (*Urges* HARRY *to sofa and he sits.*)

HARRY. All right, I'm sitting.

EDITH. Now, the nursery is on its way. They're going to rip up the floor for the radiant heating, they've knocked out the window and they're making the hole bigger for the large glass bay, the wall separating it from our room has been torn down, but they've got to put up a—

HARRY. (*He catapults himself to his feet.*) Stop!

EDITH. But I haven't finished yet.

HARRY. T'*hell* you haven't! You told me you were going to have the room *repapered.*

EDITH. They can't very well paper it, Harry, until they've finished. That will come last. I thought you'd be happy about it, dear. You told me to go ahead. You said—

HARRY. I *know* what I said. But—but you didn't give me any idea of all this. Knocking out a *wall*—putting in a *glass bay.* A new bathroom! Radiant heating! (EDITH *staggers, holds her head.*) What's the matter?

EDITH. You're yelling again. It makes me feel dizzy. I might faint—

(EDITH *sits—presses a hand to her breast, preparatory to carrying out her threat. This has its desired effect on* HARRY. *He rushes to her side.*)

HARRY. No, don't! I'm sorry—I didn't mean to yell. I was just—trying to—trying—to— (EDITH *draws a deep breath and drops hand she uses to faint.* HARRY *offers her a forgiving smile.*) Are you all right?

EDITH. I'm better. I think—

HARRY. I won't yell at you any more. I'll yell at Charlie. (*Yells.*) Charlie! (*To* EDITH.) He could have told me about all this. (*Calls out at top of voice.*) *Charlie!*

(CHARLIE *comes running, appearing at dining room entrance.*)

CHARLIE. What do you want?

HARRY. Why didn't you tell me about all this in the first place?

CHARLIE. About all what?

HARRY. About all that lumber you sent out here from the yard. That lumber stacked outside that they're using upstairs.

EDITH. Harry—

CHARLIE. I don't know anything about any lumber being sent here.

HARRY. What do you mean you don't know about—?

EDITH. (*She gently yanks at* HARRY'S *suit coat.*) Harry, that lumber came from Cooper's lumberyard. That's where I ordered it from.

HARRY. From *Cooper's!*

CHARLIE. See? You're always yelling at me for—

HARRY. Shut up! (*Sits on sofa.*) *I'm* in the lumber business, Edith. Why did you have to go to old man Cooper if you wanted lumber?

EDITH. I think you should listen to this, Harry. I did call your place first and spoke to a Mr. Henney, and I told him what I had to order and he gave me a price—But frankly it seemed a little high, so then I called Cooper's. Well, Cooper's, you know, is the only other lumberyard besides yours, Harry—

HARRY. I *know* that. Just go on.

(CHARLIE *listens very seriously, weighing the whole situation.*)

EDITH. Well, then I called Cooper's and told them about the same order—now, this is where I think you should listen, Harry—

HARRY. Believe me, I'm listening.

EDITH. Well, Cooper's price on the same lumber was *seven dollars and fifty cents cheaper*. You're a little high, Harry.

CHARLIE. (*Wide-eyed.*) I don't believe it—

EDITH. (*Raising her right hand.*) It's true!

HARRY. He means—he doesn't believe—and I can hardly believe it either, Edith—that you'd go to someone else for lumber when I could have given you all you wanted. Don't you understand? No matter what price I sell it for, I would have given it to you for *cost*. What am I talking about! I'd have given it to you for nothing.

CHARLIE. Sure. Free of charge. We'd have just padded somebody else's bill.

HARRY. (*He gives* CHARLIE *a murderous look.*) Edith—I just don't know what to say—really.

CHARLIE. Funny—old man Henney didn't tell me about it. I was standing right there next to him when he fixed up that baby carriage.

EDITH. Baby carriage, Charles?

CHARLIE. Oh, yeah. Some of the fellows had a little joke over at the yard. They wheeled in a baby carriage with a two-by-four wrapped up in a blanket. (HARRY *gives him a dirty look.*) Sort of a tribute.

EDITH. (*Chuckling.*) Wasn't that funny, Harry!

HARRY. No!

EDITH. I must tell Grace.

HARRY. No, you must not tell Grace!

EDITH. All right, dear—if you don't want me to. (*She has been struggling to unwrap the package done up in strong cord. Now she starts for the kitchen.*) I've got to get the scissors— (*She exits through dining room.*)

HARRY. Who gave you permission to tell the help down at the yard I was going to have a baby? Huh?

CHARLIE. (*Defensively.*) Well, they'd have found out by themselves anyway. A person can't have a secret baby, you know. I mean, you have to register it or something, don't you?

HARRY. I never said I wasn't going to register my own baby. I just don't need you for publicity purposes, that's all!

CHARLIE. Would you rather the whole thing leaked out through a perfect stranger?

HARRY. Any baby that takes place in this family doesn't have to be *leaked out*—by *anybody*. It's nobody's damn business!

CHARLIE. It's not normal to have a baby without people knowing it. I don't even think it's legal.

HARRY. Are you standing there telling me I'm trying to have an illegal baby? Huh?

CHARLIE. (*Defeated.*) Okay. It's your baby. Do whatever you want with it.

HARRY. That's more like it—and don't forget it! Just keep your nose out of the baby—completely!

(EDITH *re-enters with package, calling back toward kitchen.*)

EDITH. They always hung right there on that hook—(*The* MEN *pay no attention to her.*)

CHARLIE. Okay.

HARRY. Okay.

(KATE *enters wearing old pajamas, apron, one cooking glove, hair curlers, and carrying scissors.*)

KATE. Here, Mother—I found them. (EDITH *takes scissors and unwraps package.* KATE *sees the bathroom fixtures.*) Well—there's not much privacy, but at least it's different!

HARRY. Y'know—you just don't look neat for some reason.

KATE. I happen to be *working* from morning till night! (*She snaps herself around and stamps out through dining room.*)

HARRY. Where does she work—in a Chinese laundry?

EDITH. Really, Harry—you should have a little more consideration.

CHARLIE. Yeah—after all! This kind of work is new to Kate.

HARRY. What kind isn't?

EDITH. Kate is doing a wonderful job, dear. Don't forget—she was never actually domesticated. Charles—why don't you go out and say something nice to her?

CHARLIE. Yeah—that's a good idea—if I can think of something. (*He exits through dining room.*)

EDITH. (*Having unwrapped the box, holds up a baby dress.*) Harry, look! (HARRY *looks at it, aghast, and sinks slowly down onto the commode. His arms drop straight down and his right hand comes into contact with the pipe end of the commode. His fingers run over it searchingly and he realizes he's sitting on the commode. Keeping his eyes on* EDITH, *he rises embarrassedly and removes himself to the chair* R. EDITH *has been carrying on her happily unmindful conversation.*) I know it was silly of me to get it so soon. But I just couldn't resist it. Isn't it sweet—and look— (*She holds up a pink baby bonnet. He looks, glassy-eyed, and* EDITH, *finally noticing his manner, comes over to him.*) You seem tired, dear. Maybe something is troubling you??

HARRY. (*Drily.*) Maybe that's it—

EDITH. (*Off on a cloud.*) Oh, Harry—I feel so happy! It seems that a whole new world has opened up to me. Don't you feel the same?

HARRY. (*Miserably.*) I was happy in the old world—

GRACE'S VOICE. (*Calling Offstage* R.) Yoo-hoo!

EDITH. (*She crosses to front door.*) Here comes Grace!

HARRY. I'm busy— (*Crosses to desk.*)

EDITH. Come in, Grace—

(GRACE *enters buoyantly, carrying book.*)

GRACE. Hello, hello, hello! (*Sees bathroom fixtures.*) Oh, you got them. Bee-ootiful!

EDITH. As Harry always says—it's the best money can buy.

HARRY. Edith, please—from now on, forget what I always say.

GRACE. But, Harry—how exciting all this is! I saw the lumber out in the yard. And—

HARRY. Everybody in Calverton saw the lumber—and that's not all. I hope the Mayor wasn't home. If he saw those things— (*Points to the fixtures.*) out on the lawn, good-bye highway—he'll put the road on the other side of town.

GRACE. Oh, he's home, Harry.

HARRY. How do you know?

GRACE. I spoke to him. He's coming over to see you.

HARRY. (*Rises.*) He is?

GRACE. As soon as he finishes spraying his roses.

HARRY. Mad?

GRACE. Oh, no, he was real friendly. (*During the following* HARRY *wanders nervously to the front door and glances out apprehensively.* GRACE *sits on sofa. Hands* EDITH *book.*) Edith, here's that book I told you about. A little gift from me to both of you.

EDITH. (*She sits and enthusiastically pulls off wrapper. Reading title; eagerly.*) "From Here to Maternity." Oh, thank you, Grace.

HARRY. (*Draws back to them.*) What kind of a book is that? (*Snatches it from* EDITH.)

EDITH. All it is is information. I like to know the latest things, don't you, Harry?

GRACE. (*To* HARRY, *exaggeratedly devilish.*) Not that anybody could teach *you* much—

HARRY. Now listen here, Grace—we may have known each other for thirty years, but not *that* well!

EDITH. (*A bit shyly.*) Harry—don't you realize Grace is just being lively?

GRACE. (*To* HARRY; *hopelessly.*) Really, Harry—you should go to one or two foreign movies. (HARRY'S *only answer is a black look. Then, rather than make more conversation he cursorily looks through the book.*) Anyway, Edith, it's a highly recommended book.

HARRY. (*His eyes suddenly become saucer-wide as he looks at one particular page, turns it sideways, then bangs the book shut. In complete shock.*) This book is *illustrated!* (*No two ways about it.*) Grace—I won't have this thing lying around the house! (*Thrusts it back to* GRACE.) You keep it.

GRACE. What in heaven's name can *I* do with it?

HARRY. (*Significantly.*) Just keep it handy. Who knows—?

(GRACE'S *mouth drops opens as the horrible thought strikes her.* CHARLIE *enters from dining room.*)

CHARLIE. Kate said to tell you dinner will be late.

GRACE. Hello, Charlie—

HARRY. Again? I like to eat when it's *time* to eat.

GRACE. Most society people don't eat till very late, you know, Harry.

HARRY. They look it!

(*This stops that line of conversation cold.* CHARLIE *changes the subject by directing his attention to the bathtub.*)

CHARLIE. Hey, Mom, is this supposed to be a baby tub? It looks big enough for *me*.

EDITH. I don't know, Charles. I just picked it out because I liked it.

CHARLIE. Let's see— (HARRY'S *thoughts and attention*

are elsewhere as CHARLIE *steps into tub and reclines.*) Sure—I fit fine.

EDITH. Yes, you do.

GRACE. (*Rises, crosses above tub.*) It could have been made for you.

HARRY. (*Suddenly he becomes aware of* CHARLIE *reclining in the tub. He reacts.*) What are you doing in that thing with your clothes on!

CHARLIE. What do you mean with my clothes on? I'm not going to take a bath. I'm just trying it out for size. (*Slides down further and relaxes.*) This is perfect. You can just rest the back of your neck and sort of dream—

HARRY. I'll have one like it put in your office! (HARRY *has noticed something out the window.*) Here comes the Mayor! (HARRY *becomes panic-stricken. To* CHARLIE.) Get out of that thing, you idiot! (CHARLES *scrambles out of tub. Pointing at commode.*) Hide this whachamacallit! (CHARLIE *rushes to pick up commode.* EDITH *hurriedly tidies pillows.* CHARLIE *scurries aimlessly with commode, ending near closet.* HARRY *bellows.*) What are you doing??

CHARLIE. (*Helplessly.*) I don't know! I never hid one of these things before!

HARRY. Put it in the clothes closet! (CHARLIE *puts commode on top of cases in closet, follows after* HARRY *who looks out door.*) Well, well, well—here comes our good neighbor— (HARRY *turns to* CHARLIE *and sees open closet door.*) Shut the bathroom door! (CHARLIE *quickly slams it shut and crosses above sofa.* HARRY *opens door for* MAYOR.) Mr. Mayor. It's nice to see you. (MAYOR CRANE *enters carrying a single beautiful rose. The* MAYOR *has a rather superior air about him and expects everyone to cater to him and fear him.*) Come right in!

(HARRY *offers his hand but the* MAYOR *misunderstands, thinking* HARRY *is reaching for the rose.*)

MAYOR. No, no—this is not for you. It's for the bride. (EDITH *has come forward to greet him and he hands her the flower.*) I heard the wonderful news and I want to offer my congratulations.

EDITH. Thank you. (*Turns.*) You know Mrs. Kimbrough.

MAYOR. (*Crossing to sofa.*) We spoke just a few minutes ago.

EDITH. (*Passing rose under* HARRY's *nose.*) Isn't this lovely, Harry? (*He shudders.*)

MAYOR. I wanted to get here before the crowd.

HARRY. Crowd? What crowd?

MAYOR. Your well-wishers, Harry.

EDITH. You must be joking, Mayor. Grace—isn't this a beautiful rose?

GRACE. The Mayor's garden is the envy of us all.

MAYOR. Well—I protect it. And sometimes it isn't only the bugs who are after my roses—sometimes it's the passers-by.

GRACE. Oh, no—

EDITH. I think it's disgraceful.

MAYOR. Just the other night, I happened to be looking out my window and there was a young hoodlum in there.

GRACE. Really!

MAYOR. I yelled at him and when he started to run I recognized that red-headed son of Alderman Kelly.

EDITH. Oh, dear—

GRACE. I'm not surprised.

MAYOR. Next day at a meeting of the Board of Estimate I says to Kelly: "That boy of yours is very fond of my flowers, eh Alderman?" "Oh," he says, "he's just a big-hearted fellow who likes to give posies to the girls."

GRACE. Really!

MAYOR. Well, when Kelly's nephew comes up for the job of tax collector, I'm a big-hearted fellow who's going to give it to somebody else. I have ways—and means. (*Suddenly he sees the tub.*) My!

EDITH. Oh—it's for the baby.

MAYOR. Yes??

EDITH. I mean in the nursery. You probably saw the lumber out front.

MAYOR. Yes, I did. I thought maybe Harry was building a playpen for the little one—or, the twins. (*He laughs.* GRACE *joins in.*)

EDITH. Well, yes—it will cause quite a few changes.

MAYOR. It would. It would indeed. (*Again he bursts into laughter, then turns to appease* HARRY.) You'll forgive me, neighbor. I'm really filled with admiration. (*To* GRACE.) In fact, Mrs. Kimbrough, I think it's safe to say that the whole town is filled with admiration.

HARRY. The whole town?

MAYOR. News like that travels fast.

HARRY. It's a private matter.

MAYOR. Sure it is. (*Again he bursts into laughter.*)

HARRY. Well, I don't see any reason to—

MAYOR. Harry—you may cause a domestic revolution here in Calverton. You're putting the rest of us on the spot. You've become a household word with our wives.

CHARLIE. (*Inquisitively.*) Yeah! What's the word they use?

HARRY. Charlie!

MAYOR. Let me just say this, Harry. If you wanted to run for Mayor tomorrow, you'd beat the living daylights out of me. You'd get every woman's vote in Calverton. So if there are any jokes made at your expense, you can just plain put it down to jealousy. (*Rises.*) Well—I've got a meeting tonight—

EDITH. Oh, please don't hurry away—can't you stay and visit with us a—? (HARRY *puts hand over her mouth.*)

MAYOR. By the way, Harry, I feel confident that the road you want run by your place is going to pass the Board. I'm going to tell the members that you, as a young father, need a little special consideration.

HARRY. Yes. I appreciate that. I think the road will be good for the town as well as for me.

MAYOR. Right you are, we can't have too many good roads.

EDITH. Thank you for the flower.

MAYOR. My pleasure. Oh, another thing—we've got a

bassinet and quite a lot of baby stuff left over from when my grandchild was here visiting.

HARRY. Well, that's Edith's department.

MAYOR. You let me know if you want any of it.

EDITH. Thank you, Mayor.

(MAYOR *exits.*)

HARRY. Yes, thank you very much. (*He smiles.* HARRY *shuts the door, turns, and his lips frame a curse.*)

EDITH. (*Scandalized.*) Harry!

HARRY. If it hadn't been for that highway, I wouldn't have been so polite.

EDITH. But he was being nice.

HARRY. Like hell he was. He thought he was so funny. He was trying to be so smart.

CHARLIE. I can't remember whether I voted for him or not—

HARRY. You voted the straight ticket—of course you voted for him.

EDITH. I was thinking of voting for that Democrat, what's-his-name—

HARRY. Edith! We took our marriage vows as Republicans!

GRACE. (*Rising.*) Well, I think I'll just run along myself.

EDITH. You've been sweet about everything, Grace.

GRACE. Oh, I never had a better time in my life. And, Edith—we'll get together again tomorrow. Shall we?

EDITH. (*Nods.*) Good-bye, Grace— (GRACE *exits front door.* EDITH *crosses above sofa, pats back of* HARRY'S *head in passing.*) I'll go see how Kate's doing with the dinner. (*She exits through dining room.*)

HARRY. (*Grumbling to self.*) The whole town talking about me! (*Rises.*) All right. Before some other snoopy well-wisher comes in here, let's get this thing out of sight. (*Indicates bathtub.*)

CHARLIE. Gee, Dad—do we have to do it now?

HARRY. I don't want it sitting here in the living room.

CHARLIE. Well—it isn't as if it's connected!

HARRY. You know something? I don't think *you're* connected! Now grab on and let's go.

CHARLIE. (*Crossing to end of tub.*) Boy, you could have had a great military career—

HARRY. Huh?

CHARLIE. Nothing. (*They reach down and pick up tub.*) Okay, let's go.

HARRY. (*Just as he is about to lift, he stops and straightens.*) Don't you tell *me* let's go. I'll tell *you* let's go. (*Then:*) Let's go!

(*Resignedly* CHARLIE *reaches down again and they* BOTH *pick up tub.*)

CHARLIE. Where do you want it?

HARRY. You can't hide it under the sofa. Put it up in your room. You can sleep in it. (CHARLIE *stands there, shaking his head over* HARRY'S *irascibility.*) Well, what are you waiting for?

CHARLIE. I'm waiting for you to say—let's go.

HARRY. I already *said* let's go! (*Straining under the weight,* HARRY *and* CHARLIE *reach stairs and start struggling up. As* HARRY *reaches bannister with his end of tub:*) Hold it a minute—rest it here— (*Removes his tie from inside tub. They continue up stairs.*)

(EDITH *and* KATE *enter from dining room.*)

EDITH. What are you doing?

HARRY. What's it look like?

KATE. Charlie, you could very well sprain your back lifting that thing.

HARRY. (*To all.*) Nobody cares about *my* back.

EDITH. (*Considerate afterthought.*) You could easily sprain your back, too, Harry.

HARRY. Thank you—

(HARRY *and* CHARLIE *finally reach top of stairs and exit.* EDITH *looks compassionately at her exhausted* KATE *who has flopped into the chair* L. *of sofa. There is a THUD upstairs.*)

HARRY'S VOICE. Owww! Get out of here and leave me alone—*okay?*

(CHARLIE *comes hurtling from upstairs, pulling up sharp at second landing.*)

EDITH. (*Starting up stairs.*) What happened?

CHARLIE. He set that thing down on his own foot and blames it on me like everything else!

EDITH. Oh, dear—!

(EDITH *rushes upstairs to* HARRY *and exits.* CHARLIE *approaches* KATE, *looking toward top of stairs again and shaking his head.*)

CHARLIE. There's something between us that just doesn't come out right. (*Then notices* KATE'S *dejection and studies her for a moment.*) You look real tired, Kate.

KATE. Don't let my looks fool you. I'm really dead.

CHARLIE. (*Jocularly.*) Y'know—it seems like Mom is getting younger and you're getting older.

KATE. Thanks.

CHARLIE. (*Sits on sofa.*) I didn't mean it to sound exactly like that—

KATE. Well—you happen to be right. (*A seed of rebellion germinating.*) Charlie—did you ever count these stairs? There are three hundred of them. That's twenty, multiplied fifteen times running up and down dragging a vacuum cleaner and trying to cook at the same time. (*Sits beside* CHARLIE.)

CHARLIE. Gee, you must be dead, honey. But, that's what a house is.

KATE. He doesn't care how much I work—

CHARLIE. He works hard and—

KATE. He likes it. I'm just the opposite. I hate it. (*Jumps up.*) This house needs a maid!

CHARLIE. (*Pulls her down.*) Now, come on, Kate—Don't start anything.

KATE. Oh, no! Listen—Charlsey! I'm going to start something—and so are you.

CHARLIE. Me?

KATE. You. Both of us. We're going to outsmart the old bear.

CHARLIE. We are? (KATE *nods.*) How?

KATE. (*Beckons him.*) I'm going to become pregnant.

CHARLIE. Oh— Do you think that's a good idea? I mean—is it logical?

KATE. It's perfectly logical.

CHARLIE. Now, listen— We said we'd wait for the proper moment and then discuss it.

KATE. We're discussing it.

CHARLIE. You're all upset. You'll see. The work will get easier around the house. It's all a matter of getting used to it.

KATE. I'm never going to get used to it. But believe me, I'm looking forward to my labor pains.

CHARLIE. You can't have a baby in anger—!

KATE. Oh—I've given you the wrong impression. I'm going to enjoy every minute of it.

CHARLIE. Will you watch your language, please? Now, listen to me. I haven't got enough money yet for you to get pregnant.

KATE. I won't charge you a cent! (*She throws herself on him.*)

CHARLIE. (*Pushing her away.*) Kate— Do you know what you're doing? Y-y-you're going into competition with your own mother, that's what you're doing.

KATE. And you're going into competition with my father.

CHARLIE. It sounds indecent. (KATE *snuggles and nuzzles him.*) Kate! What if the folks come down!

KATE. (*She relents, untwines herself from him and rises.*) You're right, darling— (*Breathily.*) I'll see you later tonight— (*Waggles her finger at him and starts to-*

ward kitchen. At dining-room entrance she stops, turns sexily and smiles.) I'm making the roast *rare*—

(KATE *exits.* CHARLIE *mops his brow, turns front.*)

CHARLIE. Chee!

CURTAIN

ACT TWO

SCENE 2

TIME: *About noon. On a Saturday. A new hi-fi has been added. Fits flush with sill of Upstage bay window.*

AT RISE: *Front door opens and* EDITH *and* HARRY *enter.* HARRY *wears dark glasses and a hat.* EDITH *dressed smartly and full of joie de vivre. They unload packages and* EDITH *immediately delves into bag containing phonograph records.*

EDITH. Are your eyes better, dear?

HARRY. They're all right indoors. (*Takes off glasses.*) I never knew they sold so much stuff nowadays for babies.

EDITH. We didn't buy one thing that wasn't necessary.

HARRY. Most families, you know, hand baby things down.

EDITH. Well—the Mayor said we could have his things in the attic.

HARRY. The hell with his junk. What happened to all of Kate's baby things? We bought her toys, blankets, sweaters—rattles—everything a baby could ask for.

EDITH. Harry, that was twenty-four years ago.

HARRY. People making money off babies.

EDITH. (*She is preoccupied, happily shuffling through the records.*) Wait till you hear this new cha-cha record.

I heard it last night on the radio. (*Goes to hi-fi with record.*) Harry, I can't tell you how much pleasure this hi-fi set is giving me. How did you know I wanted one so much?

HARRY. I didn't until you bought it.

(*MUSIC starts.*)

EDITH. It's beautiful— (*Starts swaying to rhythm.*)

HARRY. It's lunch time. I'm hungry—

EDITH. (*She continues her solo.*) Didn't you eat?

HARRY. Where could I eat? In Kiddy-Land? At the Cradle Shop? At the Pink Di-Dee?

EDITH. Why don't you see if Kate has anything for you?

HARRY. Kate!

(KATE *enters wearing a kimono over pajamas, no makeup and cooking gloves. She's a mess.*)

KATE. What?

HARRY. What's for lunch? I'm hungry.

KATE. Lunch? I didn't expect anybody home for lunch. I thought you were going to spend the day shopping.

HARRY. What do I have to do—make an appointment to eat in my own house?

EDITH. Aren't there any left-overs in the refrigerator, Kate?

HARRY. I don't *want* any left-overs.

KATE. (*Taking a brave stand.*) Well, I just finished cleaning up in there. The kitchen's *closed.*

HARRY. Don't tell me the kitchen in this house is closed! Open it back up! (KATE *goes back to kitchen.*) And can't she put a bathrobe or something over that kimono?

EDITH. You're being cross. Come on—cha-cha-cha.

HARRY. Oh, no—no—

EDITH. Yes—yes— (*Pulls him to his feet. Starts him*

dancing.) Harry, you don't CHA when I do. It's cha-cha—cha-cha-cha—

(CHARLIE *barges in the front door.*)

CHARLIE. Hey, Dad—I've got to talk to you!

HARRY. (*Stops dancing.*) No, I don't want to. It's a silly dance anyhow.

EDITH. It is not and the exercise is very good for me. The doctor said so. Here, Charles—you show him how.

CHARLIE. (*Starts dancing with her, does it well.*) You left me in a terrible spot on that Adamson deal. Here I was stuck with it all day long and you never showed.

HARRY. Aren't you big enough to handle a simple thing like that?

CHARLIE. I can handle it all right if I only had some authority.

EDITH. Look at Charles—he's wonderful, dear. He has it from the waist down.

HARRY. I wish he had it from the *neck up*. Edith, will you please turn it off? I'm getting a dizzy headache. (*She turns it OFF.*) Now, maybe we can think.

EDITH. Would you be happier if I put on your marching record?

HARRY. I don't *want* to be happy. I just want to be *quiet*. (*To* CHARLIE.) Now, let's have it. Did you let the Adamson deal fall through?

CHARLIE. No, I didn't. I got sixteen thousand.

HARRY. Oh! Well—what are you kicking about?

CHARLIE. But I had to say you okayed it. I had to pretend I got you on the telephone. Don't you care anything about the business—staying away all day?

HARRY. I can make more money staying home cutting the spending here. It's going out faster than it's coming in. Dishwashers, deep freezers, laundry room, flowers on my desk! Grace Kimbrough has been doing nothing but fill Edith with ideas—and your wife, too. Laundry room! They're turning this house into a hotel.

CHARLIE. Don't blame my wife for any laundry room. It's to wash *your* diapers, not *mine*.

HARRY. What kind of a crack is that?

EDITH. Now, really, Charles—that didn't sound very nice.

CHARLIE. Who started it?

EDITH. That's a good question, Harry.

HARRY. I'm not interested in his good questions. I'm interested in my good answers. (*At* CHARLIE.) Now, let's get something straight around here. Who do you think is paying your salary? Huh? *Me. That's* who!

CHARLIE. Well, as far as that goes, you're not paying me enough. Remember, I went to college.

HARRY. They pay you more than I do?

CHARLIE. Look, Dad—I have a right to see the firm doesn't go bankrupt. Don't forget—when you're dead, the business goes to me.

HARRY. What do you mean "when I'm dead"?

CHARLIE. Well, let's face it—you can't last forever.

HARRY. Who says so??

CHARLIE. (*Defeatedly.*) Maybe you can—

(KATE *enters with a sandwich wrapped in wax paper.*)

KATE. (*To* HARRY.) Here's your lunch.

HARRY. (*He is repelled by odor of sandwich held out by* KATE.) What *is* it?

KATE. A sardine and onion sandwich.

HARRY. You're trying to make me sick, is that it?

KATE. What's wrong with sardines?

HARRY. I like a hot lunch—not a cold sandwich!

KATE. Would you like me to heat it up for you?

HARRY. That whole idea takes my appetite away. (*Tosses sandwich on sofa.*)

KATE. Oh, it's easy to criticize—

EDITH. That's very true, dear. Once in a while the cook likes a word of praise.

HARRY. All right—you cooked a delicious dinner last night. I can still taste it!

KATE. Thank you. Thank you so much. You're all conspiring against me, that's what you're doing! Look at me! Look at my *hands*. And my *hair*. (*Self-pityingly.*) I haven't been dressed for I don't know how long! Work, work, work! And for what? So I can work some more! *Look* at me—I'm a mess! (*They* ALL *look at her.*)

CHARLIE. (*Observantly.*) It's true. You *are* a mess.

EDITH. You're still a very pretty girl, Kate.

HARRY. At least you look *used* for a change.

CHARLIE. Kate—why don't you take an hour off from the housework and go to a beauty parlor?

KATE. (*She can hardly believe her ears.*) How *generous* of you—

HARRY. (*To* CHARLIE.) Who gave *you* permission to give her an hour off?

CHARLIE. (*Courageously.*) Now, wai——t a minute! *That* happens to be my wife!

HARRY. And *it* happens to be working in *my house!*

(KATE *looks from* CHARLIE *to* HARRY *as though she is about to lose her mind.*)

CHARLIE. (*Stands ground.*) Well, if you want to look at it that way, I can get her a job as good as this any place in town, you know!

HARRY. You *are* living in a dream world, aren't you?

EDITH. Harry—I don't think you realize how much work Kate does around here.

CHARLIE. (*He spies sandwich on sofa.*) Hey, Dad—if you don't want this sardine and onion sandwich, I'll eat it. I love them.

HARRY. *You would.*

CHARLIE. (*He takes sandwich as he comments.*) Boy, I'm glad I'm not married to you!

HARRY. And the same goes for me!

EDITH. Harry—I think we should have a little family conference.

HARRY. About what?

EDITH. Well—this is a very big house and I don't think you realize how much work there is.

HARRY. *Everything* takes work.

(CHARLIE *is eating sandwich.*)

EDITH. (*Finds courage.*) Then why can't we have a maid?

(*There is a moment of deathly silence before* HARRY'S *volcanic eruption.*)

HARRY. A *WHAT—?*

EDITH. A maid, dear. Just to help out a little. A *little?*

HARRY. There's not going to be any maid in this house invading my privacy! And that's final, Edith.

KATE. (*Distantly.*) Thanks for trying, Mother—

HARRY. (*At* KATE.) I suppose that's another idea you've put into your mother's head, huh?

(CHARLIE *has just taken a big bite of sardine and onion sandwich. He stalwartly confronts* HARRY *as he chews and crunches.*)

CHARLIE. Now, hold on there! I happen to know Kate is too smart to suggest having any maid in this house.

HARRY. (*He is repelled by* CHARLIE'S *odoriferous words.*) Would you mind not eating whatever you have to say in my face?!

EDITH. Other people have maids, who can afford it.

HARRY. I don't care about *other* people. You took care of this house, for a long time, Edith. And I never heard you complain. There's such a thing as *pride,* you know!

KATE. (*Utterly defeated.*) Don't argue, Mother—

EDITH. (*Courageously.*) Well, I'd like to complain, now!

HARRY. Please, Edith—I don't want to discuss it any more!

EDITH. Why be that way about having a maid, dear? Maybe just part time? Can't we try it that way?

HARRY. NO!

KATE. (*Vacantly.*) I told you, Mother—

EDITH. But, Harry—you've been so wonderful about everything else. The nursery—all the wonderful new things we've done. And you've enjoyed it, haven't you? Now, admit it, Harry. Dining out—going to shows. Hasn't it been fun?

HARRY. All right, Edith—you want the truth, I'll give it to you! Fun is tending to business down at the yard. Working! Not this female *nonsense.* Fun is when I go through that front gate and the men say "Morning, sir," and I say "Morning, men." Then I sit down in my office, look over the stacks of invoices, bills and contracts—*that's* fun. Charlie comes into the office and he says the foreman wants a raise, I tell him "Who doesn't!" Then I get on the phone and tell Harold Kress he'd better pay the balance of his bill—or else! Then I drive a hard bargain with Stan Dashew for a load of first-grade lumber! That's what you call *fun.* Fun isn't just something to laugh about. I like serious fun! But sitting around here, watching you make a damn fool of yourself—that's not fun!

EDITH. (*She is shocked out of her senses. She places a faltering hand to her head.*) Harry—I think I'm going to faint!

HARRY. Well, go ahead and faint! I'm going down to the lumberyard and have some fun! (*Motions to* CHARLIE.) Come on, Charlie— (HARRY *stomps toward front door and exits.*)

CHARLIE. (*Rushes to catch up with him.*) Good sandwich. I don't know what time I'll be home. 'Bye, Mom. (CHARLIE *exits. There is a short silence, then:*)

KATE. They hate us— They absolutely hate us—

EDITH. (*Sobs.*) I had no idea—

KATE. Women are fools—just plain fools—

EDITH. He said I could faint—

KATE. All men are animals!

EDITH. Now, Kate, dear, you mustn't say that.

KATE. You were never a woman to father. He turned you into a vacuum cleaner.

EDITH. He married me. That counts for something—

KATE. Charlie married me, too. Now I have to hide his pants to keep him in the same room with me.

EDITH. Kate!

KATE. Don't act shocked, Mother. It's true. In his own way, Charlie is a lot like Father. They're *both* stupid.

EDITH. I was so sure the baby would be such a blessing—

KATE. What do men care about women and babies? All they think about is themselves.

EDITH. Then why do they marry us?

KATE. They don't. We marry *them*. And then we spend the rest of our lives trying to convince them we're good enough for them.

EDITH. Kate, dear—you really shouldn't be so bitter.

KATE. Shouldn't I? Let me tell you a secret, Mother. I'm trying to become pregnant.

EDITH. (*Interjects happily.*) Oh, Kate—how wonderful!

KATE. Is it? I'm practically doing it all by myself!

EDITH. (*Embarrassed.*) It isn't nice to talk like that, Kate.

KATE. Well, it's true. And it's damn degrading!

EDITH. Charles couldn't live without you. There are *some* things I know.

KATE. That's what he told me when we got married. But it was all new then. And how do you keep a marriage new?

EDITH. You don't have to. Nothing stays new. You just have—well, you just have to keep it alive.

(*There is a thoughtful pause. Then an idea creeps into* KATE *mind and gradually begins to crystallize.*)

KATE. Mother! Do you know something?

EDITH. What—?

KATE. You said Charlie couldn't live without me, and you're right. Only he isn't aware of it. Tell me—who do you think is the last person in the world Charlie is thinking of at the moment?

EDITH. Why—why, I don't know. Charles is very occupied with business—

KATE. Exactly. And if I allow it to go on long enough, it's going to be *only* business and no Kate at all. (KATE *smiles triumphantly as she goes toward telephone. She picks up phone and starts dialing, a devilish gleam in her eye. Into phone.*) Hello, this is Mrs. Clinton. I'd like to speak to my husband, please. (*Pause.*) Well, you tell him his wife *insists* on speaking to him, no matter *how* busy he is. Thank you. (*Starts singing to self.*) K-K-K-Katie, beautiful Katie, (*Then into phone.*) Charlie? *Go to hell!* (*And with this,* KATE *hangs up.*)

EDITH. Kate!

KATE. (*She turns smilingly to her shocked mother.*) I assure you that for the rest of the afternoon, no matter how busy Charlie may be, those words will be ringing in his ears.

EDITH. But you couldn't have meant it!

KATE. (*Starts towards the stairs; stops.*) At this moment Charlie doesn't know *what* to think—but he *is* thinking of *me*. (*Continues to flow happily up the stairs.*) Now I'm going to take a nice, long luxurious bath. If anybody calls, and he happens to be my husband, tell him I'm indisposed for the rest of the afternoon.

(KATE *exits upstairs. PHONE RINGS.* EDITH *is shaken from her astonishment, rushes to answer phone.*)

EDITH. (*Into phone.*) Hello? Oh, Charles! (*Listens.*) Dear, please don't shout so. (*Listens.*) All right, I'll get her. Hold on. (*Places hand over mouthpiece; calls up.*) Kate? (KATE *appears on stairs.*) Oh, Kate!—it's Charles. He wants to talk to you. He sounds very confused and upset.

KATE. (*Smiling brightly.*) Just tell him I'm busy,

Mother. I'm taking a bath—*nude.* (KATE *pulls her head back in and closes door.*)

EDITH. (*Back into phone.*) Charles—Kate can't come to the phone. She's taking a bath—nude. (*Clamps hand to mouth and gasps at her language, then listens confused and helpless.*) Charles, I think you're being unnecessarily upset. (*Listens.*) Now, Charles, that's very foolish of you. Why should you let a few little words bother you so that you can't attend to business? Just put it out of your mind. Pretend— (*Listens.*) I'll watch every move she makes until you get home. If she leaves the house with any suitcases I'll call you immediately and then follow her. (*Listens.*) Good-bye now, Charles. Don't work too hard.

EDITH. (*She hangs up receiver, then ponders conversation. She walks away from phone, then reconsiders. After another moment of thought she goes back to phone, tentatively reaches for it, finally decides. She dials number, waits nervously. Into phone.*) Hello? This is Mrs. Lambert. I'd like to speak to Mr. Lambert. All right, I'll wait. (*She waits.*) Hello, Harry? This is Edith. (*Finds courage.*) Go to hell!

(*With this,* EDITH *clamps receiver down on cradle and pulls back with mixture of consternation and satisfaction as:*)

CURTAIN FALLS

ACT THREE

SCENE 1

TIME: *That night.*

AT RISE: EDITH *is dressed, seated at the table, waiting in the dark. She is heard sniffling.* KATE *comes down the stairs and says, reprovingly:*

KATE. Mother— (*Descends, switches on LIGHTS.*)

EDITH. I shouldn't have done it. We've gone too far. I feel like putting a light in the window or something like that.

KATE. (*Crosses to table.*) Isn't that a little old-fashioned? Anyhow, if you want to know the truth, they wouldn't be able to see it.

EDITH. What do you mean by that, dear?

KATE. Never mind.

EDITH. What do you mean?

KATE. Mother—it's bad psychology to be waiting for them. Now come on. Let's go to bed.

EDITH. Kate, tell me what's on your mind!

KATE. (*Sits at table.*) They're drunk.

EDITH. Who?

KATE. Your husband and my husband.

EDITH. How do you know?

KATE. I didn't want you to worry. While you were up taking a bath Charlie phoned. He was with Father.

EDITH. Yes—dear—

KATE. They were in some barroom—

EDITH. Oh, is that all—

KATE. And they were both drunk.

EDITH. But, Kate—neither of them drinks.

KATE. Nobody will ever be able to say *that* again.

EDITH. You're sure you're not mistaken?

KATE. Mother, they were *plastered*—

EDITH. What did Charles say?

KATE. I guess it shouldn't have come as any shock to me. He said— (*Gives bad drunk imitation.*) Calling to tell you—followed your instructions and have arrived safely in hell. (*Straight.*) Then he mumbled something about how nice the weather is down there and how friendly the people are. Then I think he suggested something about my making the same trip myself.

EDITH. Oh, I'm so worried—

(*Offstage there is sound of a CRASH as CAR screeches to a halt in the driveway. Next we hear Offstage voices of* HARRY *and* CHARLIE *as they whoop it up with laughter and burst into a drunken barbershop harmony.* EDITH *and* KATE *freeze at first, then rush to window and peek out.*)

KATE. It's worse than I thought—

EDITH. (*Shocked.*) They're holding each other up—!

KATE. Mother, let's hurry and get into our beds! We can't be here when they come in. It will only mean trouble.

(*Continued loud singing Offstage.*)

EDITH. They seem to sound happy, Kate—

KATE. Hurry up, Mother.

EDITH. (*Resolutely.*) No, Kate, I want to be right here when your father arrives. I'm going to apologize first.

KATE. You will do no such thing. The whole value of our position will be lost. Now, come on!

MAYOR. (*Offstage yelling.*) I see you out there!

HARRY. (*Offstage bellowing.*) Who are you??

MAYOR. (*Offstage yelling.*) Acting like a couple of hoodlums! Don't you know what time it is? And keep off my lawn!

CHARLIE. (*Offstage.*) Go fry an egg!

MAYOR. (*Offstage.*) Making a racket—wake up the whole street!

CHARLIE'S VOICE. Go fry an egg!

HARRY'S VOICE. He's right—go fry an egg!

MAYOR'S VOICE. If you don't quiet down I'll call an officer!

HARRY'S VOICE. Quiet down yourself!

EDITH. (*At window.*) Oh, Harry, please.

KATE. Mother, come upstairs—it's not *safe* down here.

EDITH. I don't care—it's times like this—

KATE. Mother! They're *drunk*. Come on—!

(*They run upstairs and out of sight. The yelling Offstage continues, then ceases as the* TWO MEN *reach the door. Loud rapping on door knocker. The door is shaken. Voices Offstage.*)

CHARLIE. How do you get into this joint??

HARRY. Can't find the right key—

CHARLIE. (*As he comes in window.*) I'll do it, Dad—I'll do it.

HARRY. Hurry up, will ya!!

CHARLIE. I'm comin', Dad—

(CHARLIE *opens a window and comes in. He staggers to the door and opens it.* HARRY *enters. He has a key in his hand.*)

HARRY. Hi!

CHARLIE. (*He goes to the door and yells at the* MAYOR.) Go fry an egg. (*He shuts the door.*)

HARRY. That's telling him, Charlie boy!

CHARLIE. Nobody can talk to you that way and get away with it while I'm around. Make all the noise we damn please.

HARRY. You tell 'em, Charlie boy.

CHARLIE. (*Crosses to window, leans out.*) Go fry an egg!

HARRY. You tell 'em, Charlie boy.

CHARLIE. Wonder if he likes music. (*He turns on the HI-FI.*) Having a little party, that's all.

(*By this time the MUSIC has started. He begins to dance.* HARRY *joins him; they Cha-cha.* EDITH *appears on the stairs to watch them.* KATE *comes down and pulls her back. They have changed to their negligees.*)

HARRY. I don't wanna dance no more. . . . Let's go home.

CHARLIE. (*Haughtily.*) Okay—if that's the way you fccl. (*Turns off HI-FI.*) Hey, we are home!

HARRY. (*Looking around.*) That's right! Where is everybody?

CHARLIE. Shhhhh—! Probably asleep. Let 'em sleep. Hey, buddy-buddy-boy. How about a little nightcap, huh? One more little drink—

HARRY. Where you gonna get another drink?

CHARLIE. (*Slyly.*) You'll see—

(CHARLIE *weaves his way toward dining room and disappears into the darkness.* HARRY *immediately makes himself comfortable on sofa and in a moment his eyes are closed.*)

HARRY. (*Aloud to self.*) Go to hell?!!

(*A moment later* CHARLIE *returns with a wine bottle and two water glasses.* CHARLIE *jiggles* HARRY *and the latter jerks to a sitting position.*)

CHARLIE. Wake up. I'm back.

HARRY. (*He looks around.*) What time is it?

CHARLIE. Still early.

HARRY. Well, what'd you wake me up for?

CHARLIE. (*Holds it up proudly.*) Cooking sherry. Wonderful stuff. (*Sits beside* HARRY *on sofa.* CHARLIE *pours a generous quantity in each tumbler.*)

HARRY. Y'sure that'll go good on top o' whiskey?

CHARLIE. I don't know why not. Long as you don't mix 'em. (CHARLIE *has his glass and hands* HARRY *his.*) Let's drink—

(KATE *appears quietly at top of stairs and sneaks a look over the bannister.*)

HARRY. What'll we drink to?

CHARLIE. What's a good thing to drink to?

HARRY. I don't know—I don't drink. (KATE *sneezes; alarmed that they will discover her, she exits quickly up the stairs.*) Gesundheit!

CHARLIE. Sank you. (*Gathers suit collar around neck.*) Must o' got a chill— Let's drink.

HARRY. Maybe y'ought t'be in bed.

CHARLIE. (*This suggestion horrifies* CHARLIE.) What're you tryin' t'do, kill me? You don't know what it's like up there! Wanna know a secret?

HARRY. If y'promise not t'tell anybody. (CHARLIE *raises his right hand in promise.*) Okay. What's the secret?

CHARLIE. (*He looks blurrily around to be sure they are alone, then takes* HARRY *into confidence.*) Kate wants t'get pregnant—*constantly.*

HARRY. There mus' be a kind o' virus goin' round here.

(*There is a sharp KNOCK on the door.*)

CHARLIE. Who's that?

(CHARLIE *opens the door. A young* POLICEMAN *steps in.*)

POLICEMAN. Good evening, sir.

CHARLIE. (*Crosses down to table. To* HARRY.) Telegram for you.

POLICEMAN. (*To* HARRY.) Mr. Lambert—?

HARRY. (*Crosses* U. C. *to* POLICEMAN.) Who are you?

POLICEMAN. A police officer, sir.

HARRY. Well—

POLICEMAN. There's been a complaint about disturbance of the peace.

HARRY. Disturbance of the peace?

POLICEMAN. Yes, sir—

HARRY. Well, what are you standing *here* for—why aren't you out doing something about it?

CHARLIE. Yeah, this is a quiet neighborhood.

POLICEMAN. (*He controls himself and continues calmly.*) A complaint has been registered against this house. You're making a little too much noise—you'll have to quiet down.

HARRY. Who says so?

POLICEMAN. I think tomorrow morning would be a better time to talk about that—why don't you two go to bed?

HARRY. I could have your badge for this. (*To* CHARLIE.) Take his badge number!

CHARLIE. (*He crosses around to* POLICEMAN'S L. *and presses his nose against the policeman's badge, focuses on the number.*) 7-1-3—

HARRY. The first thing you know—I'll go across the way and report you to Mayor Crane.

POLICEMAN. (*To* HARRY.) It's the *mayor* who complained about *you*, Mr. Lambert.

HARRY. The mayor?

POLICEMAN. Yes, sir.

HARRY. What's he doing up this late?

CHARLIE. 3876—

POLICEMAN. (*To* CHARLIE.) The number is 92175. Now, come on, gentlemen, I have my duty to do—and don't make it too tough for me. Just call it a night and go to bed—huh?

HARRY. The mayor sent you—? Is that what you said?

POLICEMAN. Yes, sir, he did. Good night. (*He goes, shutting the door.*)

CHARLIE. Don't worry, Dad, I got the number.

HARRY. So that's the kind of a mayor he is, a trouble-maker.

CHARLIE. (*Engraving the number on his mind.*) Seven, one, three o, ten.

HARRY. (*Beginning to get angry.*) Not only a mayor—no—he's a judge, too.

CHARLIE. Boy, is his goose cooked!

HARRY. Tried and found guilty without a jury.

CHARLIE. You're right, Dad.

HARRY. That two-bit politician trying to throw his weight around. I resent that insineration. Who do I think he is!

CHARLIE. We got to get a good lawyer.

HARRY. I got an idea—

CHARLIE. (*Raises glass.*) Drink to it.

HARRY. (*Crosses* C., *leans on back of chair. Becomes very serious and important as though making a speech.*) Mayor Crane—it gives me great pleasure to present to you an award in honor of your upholding the law so diligently. (*Crosses up to closet, opens door.* CHARLIE *gets idea and rushes to get commode.* BOTH *cross in center with it.*) We have here a little trophy with your name embossed on it. On the top of his steps, huh, Charlie boy?

CHARLIE. We could put it in his rose garden.

HARRY. It's an important award, isn't it?

CHARLIE. The *most* important—the Crane Memorial Trophy.

HARRY. Then we'll have to put it where people will see it.

CHARLIE. You're right, Dad—I give in.

HARRY. Friend and son-in-law, hold it a minute while I open the door. (*Crosses to door, opens it. As* CHARLIE *starts out with commode.*) Let me take it! I know where to put it . . . !

(HARRY *takes commode and exits.* CHARLIE *returns holding sides to suppress laughter.* HARRY *re-enters.* CHARLIE *greets him with glee, and* BOTH *embrace in a jig.*)

CHARLIE. Dad—you *use your head*. Even before anything *enters* your *mind, you use your head—!*

(*There are sounds of RUNNING Off* R. *The door is open and through it rushes the* MAYOR, *a disheveled figure, hair mussed and wearing a bathrobe hastily thrown over his pajamas. He levels a finger at* HARRY *and screams.*)

MAYOR. I saw you, Lambert! I saw you! I'm a tolerant man but you've gone too far!

HARRY. What are you talking about—?

MAYOR. I just happened to be at the window when you came sneaking over there with that thing, and you're going to pay for this! You'll pay for it!

HARRY. I don't know what you're talking about—

MAYOR. You think you're going to get that highway past your property, hey? Well, I'll show *you*. That road will be on the other side of town, that's where it will go! I'll teach you to heap your insults on me!

CHARLIE. It wasn't any insult. It was—

HARRY. You can't take that road away from me!

MAYOR. If you want favors from me, you're going about it the wrong way! I've got ways and means, let me tell you. *Ways* and *means*. That road will go past Cooper's lumberyard! (*Exits slamming door.*)

HARRY. (*After thoughtful pause.*) Look what you did to me.

CHARLIE. Me??

HARRY. Fifty thousand dollars— 'S what I just lost.

CHARLIE. Huh??

HARRY. Never get that road. An' it's all your fault.

CHARLIE. My fault??

HARRY. If it wasn't for you, all this wouldn't have happened. You and your fried eggs!

CHARLIE. You must be drunk—!

HARRY. An' how do you think I got this way? 'Cause o' you, thass how y'think I got this way!

CHARLIE. (*Defensively.*) You came in that barroom with me on your own free will.

HARRY. An' all I wanted was an Alky-Selzner f'my headache. You started all the drinkin', not me.

CHARLIE. I'm not takin' the blame for your condition jus' because you got a *weak characteristic.*

HARRY. Oh, so I'm weak—huh? Jus' lemme tell you somethin', junior. I was born *twice* the man you were, an' I'm *still* twice the man you are.

CHARLIE. (*Gathering courage.*) You make twice as much *noise* as me—*thass* all twice the man you are of me. (*Pulls* HARRY *around.*)

HARRY. Don't start any pushin' around or you'll find out somethin'— (*Pushes* CHARLIE.)

CHARLIE. Yeah? What'll I find out?? (*Pushes* HARRY.)

HARRY. You'll find out a punch in the nose, thass what! (*Pushes* CHARLIE.)

CHARLIE. Okay—you asked for it. (*Pushes him.*) Put 'em up!

HARRY. Damn right I asked for it—

CHARLIE. You want a showdown—you'll get a showdown—

(BOTH *square off, quickly clinch, trade rabbit and kidney punches.* CHARLIE *swings a roundhouse right and ends on the floor.* HARRY, *with eyes covered by arm, uppercuts air four or five times. Suddenly sees that* CHARLIE *is on the floor and takes a stance over him.* EDITH *and* KATE *have appeared from their rooms. They are horror-stricken by the sight of* CHARLIE *on the floor and* HARRY *standing victoriously over him, with still more fight left in him. They run down the stairs.*)

HARRY. Had enough? Had enough, huh? Give up??

EDITH. Harry!

KATE. Charlie!

CHARLIE. Was jus' a lucky punch—

(CHARLIE *dramatically wipes the non-existent blood from*

the corner of his mouth. KATE *is bent over* CHARLIE, *helping him to his feet, and* EDITH *stands in front of her gladiator husband, shielding any future blows with her own body.*)

EDITH. Oh, Harry, *dear. Please* don't fight! Don't fight!

(KATE *has* CHARLIE *on his feet and is making over him.*)

KATE. Father, how could you be such a bully! (*Then to* CHARLIE.) Are you all right, dear?

HARRY. It was all fair an' square.

EDITH. Are you sure *you're* not hurt?

HARRY. I took all he had.

CHARLIE. I was prob'ly hit b'low the belt. . . .

KATE. (*This seems to horrify her.*) Charlie, you weren't!

EDITH. (*Pleading.*) Harry—Charles—apologize to each other! This isn't like either one of you!

KATE. It's like *both* of them. One's as bad as the other! (*To* CHARLIE, *taking his arm.*) Now, come on upstairs—

CHARLIE. (*Pleadingly.*) I can't do it. Not in my *weakened condition.*

KATE. You-are-coming-this-instant!

CHARLIE. All right—

KATE. Now, can you make it up the stairs?

CHARLIE. (*Looks around bleary-eyed.*) Sure—where are they—? (CHARLIE *heads the wrong way and* KATE *grabs him.*) Carry me.

KATE. Oh-h-h-h, just you wait . . . !

(*Furiously,* KATE *drags her husband up the stairs and they exit. Meanwhile* EDITH *has sat* HARRY *down in a chair while rushing into kitchen for wet towel for his head.* HARRY *sits there blank-eyed, just staring off.* EDITH *hurriedly returns, places the cool damp towel on* HARRY'S *head. Then she looks beseechingly into his blank eyes.*)

EDITH. Harry—? Harry, dear—? I'm sorry about everything—the phone call. I know I shouldn't have done it. (HARRY *stares off; not looking at her.*) Please say something, Harry. (EDITH *passes her hand before his eyes; he doesn't move.*) Please—? (EDITH *puts her hand on his shoulder.*)

HARRY. Don't touch me.

EDITH. Harry, would you be happier, dear, if you yelled? Yell something, Harry.—I won't mind.

HARRY. I'm too tired to yell. Too sick an' tired. I'm too sick an' tired of everything! I'm going upstairs—(*He makes his way unsteadily toward stairs.*)

EDITH. Do you want me to come with you—?

HARRY. What for?

EDITH. We can talk about us. Maybe say some things that will make everything right again.

HARRY. Nothing's ever gonna be right again!

EDITH. Oh, Harry—how can you say that?

HARRY. 'Cause it's the truth, that's how! I was once a nice respectable citizen—now I'm the talk o' the town. I've even ruined myself with the Mayor. I'm a big fool, that's what I am. A man my age havin' a baby. Don'tcha think I know everybody's laughing at me?

EDITH. It's not true!

HARRY. Oh, it isn't, huh? (*Pulls sun glasses from pocket.*) Whatdya think I got these smoked glasses for? I didn't get 'em from any damn eye doctor! (*Tosses glasses down on floor.*) I bought 'em! To hide behind. So people wouldn't recognize me. I'm a big joke, thass what I am! Just a great big joke!

EDITH. I never suspected you felt that way—

HARRY. How'n hell could you? Y'been too busy dancin' the cha-cha-cha-cha! What kind o' idiot y'trying t'make out o' me, anyway? Look at me! Y'even finally drove me to drink. And disgrace. And ruin. (*Slowly disappears upstairs.*) You want me to yell? You're not havin' the baby—I am! All you're havin' is a picnic! Just leave me alone!

(HARRY *disappears leaving* EDITH *standing alone and shattered. She glances upstairs a couple of times then decides there's only one course to take. Controlling her tears she heads resolutely for the closet, takes out her suitcase, lays it open on floor, returns to closet and emerges with a pair of black galoshes, drops them into suitcase, goes to phone, dials, starts to write note as phone buzzes; then, into phone, tearfully:*)

EDITH. Grace?—It's Edith—everything's the matter—I'm running away. Can I spend tonight at your place? Just tonight? Right away. (*She hangs up, glances at desk but decides to leave note on table, goes to table and props note between glasses, crosses back above sofa to pick up smoked glasses, drops them into suitcase, shuts case, gets coat from closet, hitches up dressing gown under coat, picks up suitcase and hurries out front door. A few moments later* HARRY'S *voice is heard as he starts down the stairs. He is in his pajamas and has a contrite little boy sound.*)

HARRY. (*Tentatively.*) Edith—? (*Comes down to second landing, looks over rail.*) Edith? Don't be mad, Edith. (*Starts down again.*) I didn't mean everything I said—just some of it— (*With no response, he comes all the way down and heads into dining room.*) Where are you, Edith? (*Comes out and crosses above sofa.*) It's me—Harry. (*With growing concern, peeks into partly open closet, shuts closet door, goes to front door, opens it, slightly angrily.*) Edith—don't play games! (*Shuts front door, crosses down toward table, spies note, reads it, his eyes widening with disbelief. Horrified, he shouts wildly upstairs to* KATE *and* CHARLIE.) Kate! Charlie! Drop everything and come down here! D'ya hear me? (*Sits down, rereading note.*)

(KATE *and* CHARLIE *come rushing down the stairs in nightgown and pajamas, struggling into bathrobes.*)

KATE. What is it??

HARRY. She's run away!

CHARLIE. Who's run away?

HARRY. (*He thrusts note at* KATE.) Here—read this!

KATE. (*She takes note and reads to self.*) Oh, no—!

CHARLIE. What's it say?

KATE. (*Reads aloud.*) "Since the day I told you I was going to have a baby, everybody has been unhappy. So now I'm going away. Maybe you will all learn to smile again. Nobody has smiled in a long time. Good-bye—" (KATE *looks up from note, stunned.*)

HARRY. (*Recalls.*) I smiled yesterday—

KATE. Well, we can't just stand here moaning. We've got to *do* something!

HARRY. You're right! (*Rushes to phone and dials operator.*) Hello, operator? Gimme the police! This is an emergency!

KATE. Now try to speak plainly, Father.

CHARLIE. So you're gonna turn in your own wife—! Boy-oh-boy—

HARRY. (*Into phone.*) Hello, police? I wanna report a missing person! Stop all busses, trains and airports! Don't let anything leave this town! There's a woman in no condition to— *Huh?* Never mind my name, I don't want this in the newspaper! (KATE *groans.*) Now you listen t'me—this happens t'be my wife! Y'can't miss her. She's an *old, pregnant woman!*

CHARLIE. What're y'tryin' t'make her sound like?

KATE. Mother isn't that *old,* and she isn't that pregnant!

HARRY. (*Back into phone.*) Hold it! Look for a woman who's not very old an' just a little bit pregnant. (*Listens; then:*) You have? Well, hold her there! Don't let her get away! (*Slams down receiver.*) They just picked up a woman walkin' the streets a little while ago! I'm goin' down t'claim her!

(HARRY *dashes to door.* KATE *grabs his hat and coat from closet. She clamps hat on his head as he rushes to-*

ward front door, struggling into his coat over pajamas.)

KATE. Father, you're in no condition to drive!
CHARLIE. *I'll* drive you.

(*And as* CHARLIE *rushes forward he runs into* HARRY'S *left arm emerging from coat sleeve, and falls. From his prone position on the floor* CHARLIE *dizzily looks about.*)

KATE. Oh, give me strength! (*She grabs coat and runs after* HARRY, *leaving door open.*)
CHARLIE. Wha' happened—? (*He struggles to his feet, having lost sense of direction, looking blurrily around.*)

(*Now we hear sound of Offstage voices of* HARRY *and* KATE *as they scream at each other.*)

KATE'S VOICE. Father—get out from behind that steering wheel!
HARRY'S VOICE. There's no time t'waste!
KATE'S VOICE. You're just going to kill yourself!
HARRY'S VOICE. Lemme alone! Where's the gas pedal? Lemme alone, I say!
KATE'S VOICE. Now, you just sit there—*I'm* going to drive!

(*We hear sound of CAR MOTOR start up.*)

CHARLIE. Nobody cares 'bout me— That's for sure—
HARRY'S VOICE. Use the bright lights! Sound the sirene! What're y'waiting for?

(*Now we hear sound of HORN being depressed, undoubtedly by* HARRY.)

KATE'S VOICE. Father, will you take your hand off that horn!

(*Sound of CAR as it backs out of driveway and finally diminishes in the distance.* CHARLIE *listens, then ambles below the coffee table.*)

CHARLIE. Mom, wherever you are, my heart's with you! Thass all I got to say. Somebody finally broke outa here—'scaped t'freedom! Thass what I shoulda done long time ago. If I'da known, I'da run away with you.

(*Sharp knock on open door. The* POLICEMAN *strides in.*)

POLICEMAN. Now—look!

CHARLIE. He's not here.

POLICEMAN. Yeah—yeah—I'm trying to be nice about this, but the mayor's getting sore! Now, you got to cut it out!

CHARLIE. Well, let me tell *you* something, Number 7 2—zero—

(*The* MAYOR *enters in pajamas, bathrobe and slippers.*)

MAYOR. I'll take care of this.

POLICEMAN. Mr. Mayor, I was just—

MAYOR. (*Authoritatively.*) O.K. Go back to your beat —leave him to me.

POLICEMAN. Thank you, sir— (*He exits.*)

MAYOR. Screaming and yelling in the middle of the night—carrying on like hoodlums! This house ought to be quarantined. And let me tell you something—!

CHARLIE. And let me tell *you* something. You just lost a vote.

MAYOR. You and your father-in-law have lost more than that, my friend. You've lost where it hurts—right in the pocketbook!

CHARLIE. (*Realizing.*) Yeah—you're right, Mayor. That's where it does hurt. Right in the lumberyard—

MAYOR. I was trying to be nice to you—trying to be a decent neighbor. I was doing my best—!

CHARLIE. (*Devising a scheme.*) Only you made one mistake . . .

MAYOR. Harry Lambert is going to regret this night, I can tell you—!

CHARLIE. That's the mistake you made. He didn't do it!

MAYOR. Didn't do what? He insulted me—he—!

CHARLIE. No, he didn't. I'm gonna confess to you. It was *me*— You just got us mixed up, that's all—

MAYOR. No, I did not. I saw him sneak across my lawn and I heard him yell "go fry an egg" and then he yelled at me "shut up!"

CHARLIE. No, that was *me—I* yelled at you "go fry an egg" and he yelled at *me* "shut up!" He says you'll wake up the mayor and I'll never forgive you an he says turn off that music, but I wouldn't do it. He wouldn't have music in the middle of the night—not even in the *daytime*. He *hates* music. And then I got so mad at him that I says I'll show him, and that's when I came over and decorated your porch. (*Crosses to chair* L.)

MAYOR. (*Cross after him.*) But Harry Lambert was *drunk*—he was *drunk—!*

CHARLIE. (*Sits.*) Yes, he was. But that's my fault too! He thought he was drinking alka seltzers.

MAYOR. (*Sternly.*) My boy—just now—somebody drove a car out of here shouting and carrying on—!

CHARLIE. That's what I'm trying to tell you about, Mayor— There's been a tragedy.

MAYOR. What do you mean?

CHARLIE. Mom—

MAYOR. What about her?

CHARLIE. (*Exaggerated concern.*) She's lost. Run away. You'll read about it in the paper tomorrow.

MAYOR. Are you sober enough—?

CHARLIE. I'm sober now. Ever since you came in. That's why I confessed to you. Mom's all alone out there somewhere— (*Starts to blubber.*) Dad's headin' a search party lookin' for her. And it's all my fault.

MAYOR. (*Considers.*) This always seemed a happy home—

CHARLIE. It was. Except nobody smiled. And now

Dad's going to feel like he's losin' everythin', with Mom going like this and the highway all at the same time. An' it's all my fault—

MAYOR. (*Compassionately.*) Well, in that case, I'm sorry I made a mistake. I'll say no more.

CHARLIE. Say whatever you want, Mayor.

MAYOR. No, I'll just consider what happened a childish, high-school prank—

CHARLIE. (*Looks up; specifically.*) College.

MAYOR. I'm sure Mrs. Lambert will turn up all right—

CHARLIE. I'm never going to take another drink as long as I live.

MAYOR. And as far as the highway is concerned—I was speaking in anger—you just tell Harry not to worry. Tell him I understand. Tell him everything is O.K.

CHARLIE. I'll tell him—

MAYOR. (*Crosses to door.*) I'll come over and straighten things out in the morning.

CHARLIE. And, Mayor—try and get some sleep. (MAYOR *exits.*) Always takin' the blame for everything. Well, this's my last "blame." From now on I'm gonna be independent. Everything's gonna be my *own* fault! (*Tosses down sherry and savors its effect.*) I don't know why I didn't start drinkin' sooner. It clears my head.

(*At this moment* GRACE *pokes her head in from dining room entrance and looks surreptitiously around.*)

GRACE. (*Forced whisper.*) Charlie—? (*Startled,* CHARLIE *gapes at her.*) Are you alone? (CHARLIE *now looks about to be sure; nods, then:*)

CHARLIE. Yeah, I'm alone but—

GRACE. Good!

CHARLIE. Grace—I'm a married man!

GRACE. Charlie—you idiot! (GRACE *crosses back to dining room and beckons.*) It's all right.

(EDITH *now enters from dining room.*)

CHARLIE. (*Rushes to her.*) Mom! Oh, we found you—Oh, Mom. (*Throws his arms around her.*)

EDITH. Charles—I'm so ashamed—

GRACE. Never mind that talk! (*Sternly.*) Edith!

EDITH. Yes, Grace, I know—

GRACE. Remember what I told you. No apologies—

EDITH. I will. I'll remember—

GRACE. Now let's get organized. Charlie—where are the others? Do they know?

CHARLIE. Oh, sure—they've gone to the police station—

EDITH. The police station!

(*Sound of CAR skidding to a stop.*)

CHARLIE. Sure. Well, I guess they're coming back—

GRACE. (*To* EDITH.) Edith—it's much better if they don't find me here—Charlie, you keep your mouth shut.

CHARLIE. I always do—I—

GRACE. (*To* EDITH.) And remember—no apologies. I'll call you tomorrow. (*She goes* L.)

(HARRY *and* KATE *enter* R.)

HARRY. Idiots! All of them! I'm looking for a pregnant woman and they give me a vagrant woman! How could they think that old drunk was my wife?

KATE. Just be thankful they let you go! They almost locked *you* up, you know.

HARRY. That'll be the day when they lock up Harry M. Lambert! (*Spies* EDITH; *his face lights up.*) Edith—!

EDITH. Harry—!

(*Impulsively* BOTH *start to rush toward each other and embrace with joy, but he catches himself.*)

HARRY. Where the hell have you been? You almost had me worried!

KATE. (*She crosses in to sofa.*) Oh, Mother—you had us frantic!

HARRY. All right, Edith—now explain your actions! What was the meaning of that note? Did you think it would be fun to play a little game of hide and seek, is that it? I want a firm answer from you, Edith!

KATE. (*Crosses to* HARRY.) Father—let's just be thankful mother is here.

CHARLIE. (*Shakes head hopelessly. Crosses to table, sits.*) You should've kept on going, Mom. . . .

EDITH. (*She meets the challenge and takes a dignified stand.*) Harry—everything I said in that note I meant. I'm sorry about the running away part, I realize now that was foolish. But at the moment I just didn't know what else to do. You were so upset—and the baby and I were the cause of it all. (*Squarely; courageously.*) But there's one thing you've got to face, Harry. *You* impregnated *me* —*I* didn't impregnate *you*.

HARRY. (*Staggered.*) Edith! The *children* are listening!

KATE. Father, we're all very well acquainted with the facts of life.

(KATE *and* CHARLIE *exchange cold glances.*)

EDITH. There's really nothing to be ashamed of, Harry— Everybody knows sex.

HARRY. There are certain things you don't shout to the rooftops!

EDITH. (*Pleading.*) But I just can't keep apologizing for my condition, dear. To you, or to anyone. I'm *pregnant, you* did it, and you've *got* to *face* it. Would you be happier dear, if someone else was the father? For instance, Mr. Thorgenson?

(*All eyes suddenly stare incredulously at* EDITH.)

HARRY. (*Almost afraid to ask.*) Who's—Mr.—Th-Th-Thorgenson—?

EDITH. (*Innocently.*) Our garbage man. (*Now aware of shocked reaction.*) Heavens, there's nothing to be concerned about—believe me. We were just good friends Tuesdays and Fridays. In fact, since we got our garbage disposal, I don't see him at all any more. Don't you understand? I was just making an example.

(EVERYBODY *is relieved. Then, at the nadir of his endurance,* HARRY *looks closely at her, crosses around to her* L., *looks again, then* HARRY *wearily slumps down in chair.*)

HARRY. This has been the longest day of my life—

EDITH. (*Compassionately.*) Harry, you're just not used to being up so late, that's all.

KATE. (*Wearily.*) Why don't we all do the sensible thing and get some sleep? Who knows? Maybe in the morning we'll find out this was all a horrible dream.

HARRY. Mayor Crane isn't going to turn out to be any dream— (*Defeated.*) I worked hard for that highway—pulled wires—spent a small fortune on business men's lunches—eleven Merry Xmas presents—

CHARLIE. Don't worry about it—

HARRY. Worry!

CHARLIE. I took the blame—

HARRY. You what?

CHARLIE. He was over here again after you left—I told him I was the one that—you know—

HARRY. But he *saw* me—

CHARLIE. It was dark—now he thinks it was *me*. Tomorrow he's coming over to apologize to you—

KATE. (*Shocked.*) You took the blame for everything?

EDITH. But why should you do a thing like that, Charles? Is that right, Harry?

HARRY. Of *course* it's right—!

CHARLIE. I did it for the good of the firm. I saved you $50,000 but I'm not asking for a raise. I'm *quitting*. I'm going someplace else where I'll be appreciated!

KATE. You are *too* asking for a raise!

HARRY. Hold it! Nobody's gonna say I don't appreciate a piece of smart thinking. You can *have* a raise—

CHARLIE. I don't *want* just a raise— I want some *authority*—

EDITH. Why don't you be nice, Harry? Give him some authority. It's such a big yard—isn't there enough for both of you?

KATE. Don't you think it's about time, Father? After all, when Charlie first went to work for you it was understood that someday he'd get a partnership.

EDITH. (*Almost accusingly.*) I remember that, Harry.

(*There is a moment of silence, then:*)

HARRY. All right— (*To* CHARLIE, *reluctantly.*) Maybe you've earned it. When you get down to your office tomorrow have your name printed on your door.

CHARLIE. I haven't *got* a door!

HARRY. *Get* a door!

KATE. (*Rushes to* CHARLIE. *Filled with joy.*) Oh, Charlie—!

EDITH. (*Rushes to* CHARLIE.) Oh, Charles—congratulations, dear—congratulations!

(CHARLIE *stands there triumphant as* EDITH *and* KATE *embrace him with kisses and ad libs of "Congratulations," etc.* HARRY *remains alone and outside, the forgotten man.*)

HARRY. What are you congratulating *him* for? After all, *I'm* the one who just lost everything. (*With this,* EDITH *and* KATE *turn their affections on* HARRY.)

EDITH. And congratulation to you, Harry!

KATE. Oh, Father! You're just a great big wonderful doll!

HARRY. (*Exaggerated shyness.*) Thank you.

CHARLIE. My congratulations, too, Dad. (HARRY *smiles, extends hand.* CHARLIE *approaches* HARRY *with swagger and expanded chest. Takes* HARRY'S *hand and pumps it heartily.*) I'll have the lawyer draw up the legal papers in the morning. Fifty-fifty.

HARRY. (*He yanks his hand from* CHARLIE'S *grasp.*) Fifty-forty!

CHARLIE. (*Won't quibble; largely.*) All right, if that's the way you want it. Believe me, you won't regret it. From now on you can take life easy. Relax. Enjoy yourself. *You've—got—me!*

EDITH. (*Brightly.*) Did you hear that, dear?

HARRY. (*"Nods" miserably.*) *I've—got—him.*

CHARLIE. (*With a sigh of finality and satisfaction.*) Well, I guess things are a little diff'rent now, huh, Kate? Let's get up to bed. (*Going upstairs.*) Good night, Mom —good night, Dad.

EDITH. Good night, dear.

HARRY. (*Still trying to figure out what has happened.*) 'Night—

CHARLIE. You must be pretty tired, huh, Kate?

KATE. Not that tired, dear.

CHARLIE. (*In full charge, now.*) Kate—tomorrow I want you to go out and start finding us our own house. And we're going to have a *cleaning* woman three times a week. I can't bear having you look like a drudge any more. (KATE *follows* CHARLIE *up the stairs. When they reach top,* CHARLIE *turns and looks down.*) *Harry—?* Thanks a lot!

HARRY. You're welcome!

(CHARLIE *and* KATE *exit.*)

EDITH. Did you hear what Charles just said, dear? About getting their own home and everything?

HARRY. I heard all right! Now that he's a big business man he's going to try to make me look *cheap,* that's his idea. (*Scoffingly.*) A cleaning woman three times a week— (*Then; resolutely.*) Edith? You're gonna have a maid—with a *uniform.*

EDITH. (*Incredulously.*) Harry—!

HARRY. The best maid money can buy!

EDITH. That's very thoughtful of you, Harry—but

with just the two of us now, I really don't need a full-time maid.

HARRY. I'm not taking "No" for an answer, Edith. (*Considers further.*) Besides—I'm not forgetting your condition. This is a big house, you know. And— Well, you're not as young as you look, Edith.

EDITH. That's a nice thing to say, Harry— Do you really think I look young?

HARRY. (*Reluctantly.*) Well—you always had a pretty face. I've noticed that.

EDITH. Harry—you're so romantic—

HARRY. (*Passing it off.*) Awwwwww—

EDITH. Oh, yes, you are. Don't you try to squirm out of it.

HARRY. Well—

EDITH. See? You admit it.

HARRY. (*Shyly.*) Sometimes—maybe. I'm pretty young for my age, y'know—

EDITH. Of course you are. We're both young in a way— That's why having this baby is so wonderful! It means there's life in you, and—there's life in me. . . . We're still part of what makes things grow. (*Thinks.*) That should be a proud thought, Harry—

HARRY. (*Considers; then:*) Yeah. Y'know something, Edith! (*Considers further.*) Our son is going to need a good name. Something *solid.*

EDITH. I've sort of always liked "John."

HARRY. (*Tries the name.*) John. John Lambert. That sounds good. It needs something else, though.

EDITH. How about John F. Lambert?

HARRY. That's it! John Fitzgerald Lambert. Republican President of the United States!

EDITH. That sounds so wonderful—!

HARRY. (*Then a dark thought strikes him.*) You don't think being a Protestant will hurt his chances, do you?

EDITH. I'm sure any son of yours, Harry, can overcome a thing like that.

HARRY. (*After some thought.*) Yeah. Y'know, Edith—maybe it'd be better if we just named him Harry M.

Lambert, Junior. There's something about it that makes it sound more important to me.

EDITH. I like that, too, Harry—

HARRY. And that would make me Harry M. Lambert, *Senior*. It's a good way to be remembered. . . .

EDITH. (*Rests her head against his chest. Lovingly.*) Who could ever forget you, dear?

(*And as* HARRY *proudly raises his head:*)

CURTAIN FALLS

(NOTE: *The following alternate ending may be used if desired.*)

HARRY. (*Shyly.*) Sometimes— Maybe . . . I'm still pretty young for my age.

EDITH. Of *course* you are. We're both young in a way. . . . That's why having this baby is so wonderful! (*Thoughtfully.*) It means there's life in you, and—and there's life in me. . . . We're still part of what makes things grow. . . . (*Thinks.*) That should be a proud thought, Harry.

HARRY. (*Considers.*) Y'know something, Edith? Sometimes you make good sense. (*Considers further.*) Our son is going to need a good name. Something *solid*.

EDITH. (*Hesitantly.*) I haven't wanted to bring this up, dear—but what if our son turns out to be a girl?

HARRY. No son of mine is going to turn out to be a girl!

EDITH. (*Obligingly.*) If you say so, dear. (*Then, after a thought.*) You know—I think Harry would be a nice name for a boy.

HARRY. (*Quick judgment.*) Harry? Naw—it doesn't have— (*Realizes.*) Oh, *Harry*. Like *me*. (*Brightens.*) Yeah—it sounds sort of important.

EDITH. I've always thought so. Harry M. Lambert, Junior—and Harry M. Lambert, Senior.

HARRY. (*Proudly.*) Little Harry and—*big* Harry!

EDITH. (*Lovingly.*) My two men. . . . (*With this,* EDITH *embraces* BIG HARRY *and:*)

CURTAIN FALLS

FURNITURE PLOT

Sofa (6 ft.)
Small coffee table (oval-shaped)
Large desk (practical—bookcase above)
Desk chair (straight back)
Telephone table
Living-room table (circular—3 ft. diameter)
2 table chairs (straight-back—yellow upholstered seats)
Small end table (circular)
3 armchairs (open back for two used with sofa)
Large wing-back chair
Dining-room table (square—4 ft.)
4 dining-room table chairs
Small magazine table
Hall table (rectangular—folding top)
Small wall table (dining room)
Black telephone
Small rectangular stool
4 sofa pillows
Medium wall clock (pendulum type)
3 table lamps
Floor lamp
Wicker wastebasket
Magazines (under coffee table—end table—on magazine table)
4 small pictures (over hall table)
6 small pictures (around clock)
Green leaf plant (on hall table)
Large mahogany hi-fi set

PROPERTY PLOT

ACT ONE

Scene 1:

Silver serving tray
4 maroon-colored glasses
Pitcher pink lemonade
Old-fashioned pocket watch
White blouse (pressed—on hanger)
Unpressed white shirt
Hip-high fishing boots
Hammer
Wrench
Sewing basket with blue shirt, needle, thread and Edith's glasses
Towel
Safety razor
Soiled white shirt (Harry)
Pair trousers, sweater, jacket (to be carried only)

Scene 2:

Playing cards (pre-set first scene)
Vogue magazine
Keys (on key ring)
3 bank books
Check book
Dish towel
Unopened food can
Cigarette lighter

ACT TWO

Scene 1:

House blueprint
Pocket watch
Band-aids
Cooking glove
Book (titled "From Here To Maternity" in wrapper)
Single yellow rose
Bathtub (fibre glass)
Commode (with seat covers)
Scissors

Scene 2:

Hi-fi set
Assorted packages (from baby shops)
Several rattles
1 pacifier
Dark glasses (Harry)
LP in sleeve (in record envelope) "Cha Cha"
Sandwich in wax paper wrapper

ACT THREE

Large front door key
Cooking sherry bottle
2 plain drinking glasses
Slightly damp dish towel
Woman's medium size blue suitcase
Black high heel galoshes
Secretary size note paper pad (bond weight)
2 pencils
Harry's top coat—hat
Edith's top coat
Kate's top coat

LIGHTING PLOT

ACT ONE

Scene 1:

It is a summer Sunday—about noon. Bright sunlight is pouring through the bay windows, front door, hall window and dining-room windows—all playing areas are brightly lit including the upper level of the staircase. Sunlight is bright upon the houses opposite which can be seen vaguely through the windows.

Scene 2:

It is the next day—around six thirty in the evening. Lighting is the same as Scene 1.

ACT TWO

Scene 1:

It is a few days later—almost six o'clock in the evening.
Lighting is the same as the previous two scenes.

Scene 2:

It is Saturday—about noon.
Lighting is the same as the preceding scenes.

ACT THREE

It is late that night—about eleven o'clock. Moonlight is streaming through the bay windows, front door and hall window and dining-room window. A shaft of light from the upstairs level lights up the staircase area. Edith is in vague silhouette at the table.
When Kate descends and switches on the lights the downstage areas are all well-lit. The front door area is at a slightly lower level and the dining room is low-lit from the living-room spill. At the switch-on the table lamps on the desk, telephone table and hall table, and the floor lamp at the bay windows go on.

COSTUME PLOT

ACT ONE

Scene 1:

EDITH:
Navy dress, apron, heavy sweater, navy shoes, hairpiece

HARRY:
Dark brown suit, white shirt, brown figure tie, black socks, black shoes

KATE:
Mustard robe, lavender-white pajamas, slippers, blue dress, plaid coat, shoes, purse to match

CHARLIE:
Light brown sport coat, gray slacks, red tie, light blue shirt

JAMES:
Dark gray suit, red bow tie, white shirt, black shoes

GRACE:
Plum suit, printed blouse, black purse, black gloves, plum hat, black shoes

Scene 2:

EDITH:
Green suit, pink blouse, black feathered hat, black gloves, black shoes, black purse

HARRY:
Dark brown cardigan, red print tie, same pants, same shoes

KATE:
Blue dress (same sc. 1), light beige shoes

CHARLIE:
Gray slacks, black tie, brown stripe sport coat, light brown shirt, brown shoes

ACT TWO

Scene 1:

EDITH:
Electric blue dress, black shoes

HARRY:
Brown suit, tan shirt, brown print tie, black shoes

KATE:
Pink-white pajamas, pink printed apron (unironed), large cooking glove

MR. FOLEY:
Long sleeve undershirt, shirt, sweater, overalls, workshoes, felt hat

GRACE:
Beige suit, tan blouse, tan purse, tan gloves, brown shoes

MAYOR (no coat):
Gray suit with vest, black shoes, white shirt, plain tie, black socks, dark blue cardigan

CHARLIE:
Glen plaid suit, gray cardigan, solid blue tie, black shoes

Scene 2:

EDITH:
Yellow suit, yellow hat, tan shoes, tan gloves, tan purse

HARRY:
Gray suit, black and white print tie, black shoes, gray felt hat, dark glasses

KATE:
Printed kimono, pink nightgown, slippers

CHARLIE:
Same sport coat as sc. 1, Act I, stripe tie, light brown slacks, light brown shirt, brown shoes

ACT THREE

EDITH:
Pink robe, green nightgown, pink slippers, mustard topcoat

HARRY:
Pajamas, green leather house shoes, navy blue topcoat, light green rainhat

KATE:
Gold dress, pink nightgown, slippers, turquoise robe

POLICEMAN:
Blue uniform, black Sam Browne belt, hat, white shirt, black tie

MAYOR:
Bathrobe, striped pajamas, slippers

GRACE: Same as Act II
Add plaid topcoat

CHARLIE: Same clothes as Act I, Sc. 2 change to:
Light blue pajamas, brown bathrobe, slippers

SOUND PLOT

Music may be used to introduce each scene and act as a bridge between the scenes of Act I and Act II. The time allotted for each of these sequences is approximately one minute.

1. Curtain riser—starts 45 secs. before curtain which rises on cymbal crash.
2. Pipe banging—off stage left (live)
3. "Faint" music and bridge into Sc. 2.
4. Intro music into Act II, Scene 1 (which segues into:)
5. Hammering (carpenters upstairs)
6. Guitar slur on "Roast Rare" into bridge into Scene 2
7. Cha Cha Music
8. Car door slam—car leaving
9. Telephone rings (live)
10. Intro music into Act III
11. Car arrives—doors slam
12. Cha Cha Music
13. Phone buzzes (3)
14. Car doors slam—motors start—horn
15. Car arrives—doors slam
16. Cha Cha Music (Playout)

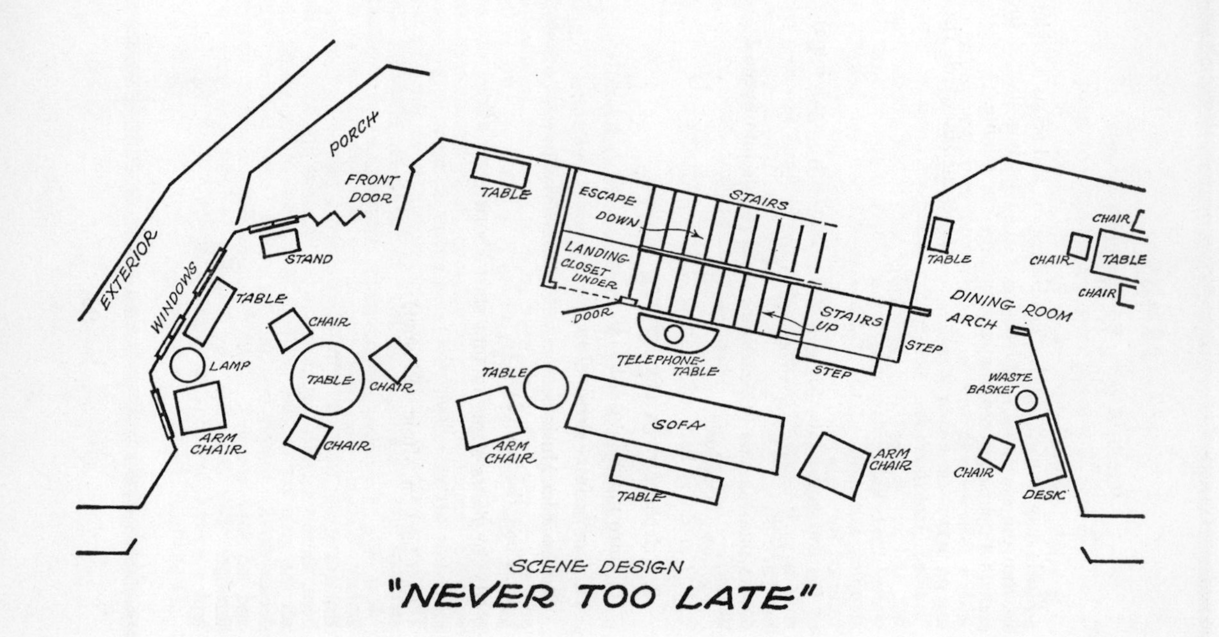

SCENE DESIGN

"NEVER TOO LATE"

JANUS

Farce. 3 acts. By Carolyn Green.

3 men, 2 women. Interior. Modern costumes.

If you're looking for a sparkling, sophisticated vehicle for an advanced group *Janus* is tailor-made for you. It's the story of the respectable wife of a West Coast shipping tycoon who spends a couple of months each summer in Greenwich Village with a married man who is a prep school professor, collaborating on sexy, best-selling historical novels under the pen name of "Janus." Unexpectedly, the tycoon husband drops in to see her, and just as he arrives the teacher arrives too, via the dumbwaiter from his upstairs apartment. There is some adroit sidestepping and then, to add to the complication and hilarity, an Internal Revenue man turns up to investigate the income taxes of the collaborators. Although the husband discovers "all," the wife is so irresistibly charming that the husband can only take her back home. After all, it isn't every man who suddenly discovers that his wife is America's most successful contemporary novelist—even though the mistress of another man.

(Royalty, $50-$25.) Price, $1.25.

THE DESK SET

Comedy. 3 acts. By William Marchant.

8 men, 8 women. Interior. Modern costumes.

Shirley Booth had them rolling in the aisles in this comedy—and any audience that has ever set foot in an office door will love it. The "desk set" in this case is a group of girls in the reference department of a radio and TV network whose jobs are suddenly threatened when an efficiency expert starts installing electronic brains (Emmaracs, or Emmy) around the premises. The first Emmy, in the Payroll Department, promptly goes berserk and fires everyone in the joint, including the president. The "desk set," with their encyclopedic memories—and especially Bunny Watson, who was played by Miss Booth, gives the Emmys a real battle of wits. And in the midst of all this mayhem, there's a typical, slightly tipsy Christmas office party when all the girls get to kiss the boss and some of the young men decide finally to tell him off. Of course, the "desk set" wins and no jobs are lost. There's a nice little romance running through *"The Desk Set;* the dialogue is brisk, the pace fast; and a good time should be had by all.

(Royalty, $50-$25.) Price, $1.25.